REVISED EDITION

Experimental Research in Music:

Workbook in Design and Statistical Tests

Edited by

CLIFFORD K. MADSEN

Florida State University
Tallahassee, Florida

and

RANDALL S. MOORE

University of Oregon
Eugene, Oregon

CPC **CONTEMPORARY PUBLISHING COMPANY**
508 ST. MARY'S STREET, RALEIGH, N.C. 27605—(919) 821-4566

Contents

Preface

This programmed workbook is designed to accompany *Experimental Research in Music* or may be used independently. It contains five programs which may be read in conjunction with the text or used to supplement other research requirements. Each program is designed to clarify basic concepts necessary for experimentation in music.

A Programmed Guide to Closed Systems takes the reader through abstract concepts, such as, transfer, sets, and modes of inquiry. The program on Mill's Canons elucidates the five basic designs from which all experimentation comes. Musical examples are included for each canon.

Selected Research Designs and Statistical Tests presents a concise overview of experimental designs and related statistical tests. This program utilizes many musical examples to help the music researcher make transfers from the cryptic, experimental symbols.

The Programmed Guide to Statistics covers some of the basic rationale, assumptions and formulas used in a formal study of statistics. The concluding program provides numerous examples of specific statistical tests with step-by-step procedures for computation to prepare the experimenter in music with the necessary skills for *independent* evaluation of research.

The programs found in this workbook were initially written by graduate students to enlarge and clarify concepts relating to experimental research in music. Appreciation of that special type not confined to scholarship or even competence is extended to these special people. It is they to whom many researchers will be grateful for that unique ease of understanding and illumination that is only gained by progressing through and mastering an excellent program.

I am indebted to the Literary Executor of the late Sir Ronald A. Fisher, F.R.S., to Dr. Frank Yates, F.R.S., and to Oliver and Boyd, Edinburgh, for permission to reprint Tables B and G from their book *Statistical Tables for Biological, Agricultural and Medical Research*.

C.K.M.

I _____

A Programmed Guide to Closed Systems

This programmed guide attempts to facilitate the understanding of "Closed Systems" found in Chapter Six of *Experimental Research in Music*. Specific ramifications for the music student are intended in order to expand and clarify the concept of closed systems.

INSTRUCTIONS

Read through the material carefully. In order to derive the greatest benefit from the technique utilized here, you should formulate your response fully before *exposing* the correct answer. A piece of paper may be used to shield the correct answers. A written response is not generally required. Research has shown that covert responding—i.e., thinking—is just as adequate and far less time-consuming. This material is completely individualized and you may work through at your own pace and are free to go back at any time to review frames. Each frame is separated from its answer by a line down the page. Answers are always found in the right margin of the page, *but* in the margin box right *below* the frame or adjacent to the next frame. That is, the answer to every frame is right beside the next frame down.

Begin

CLOSED SYSTEMS

1. A closed system is a group of objects, symbols, or ideas which are intrinsically consistent (i.e., have constant internal relationships) but are extrinsically invalid (i.e., lose intrinsic consistency when applied to other phenomena). **No Response Required**	
2. Man's use of closed systems has aided his conceptual processes and facilitated his organization and classification of the external world. **No Response**	
3. A group of objects, symbols or ideas which are intrinsically consistent but extrinsically invalid are known as a _____ _____ .	
4. A closed system may be a group of symbols which are intrinsically _____ but extrinsically invalid.	Closed System
5. A closed system is a group of objects, symbols or ideas which are intrinsically _____ but extrinsically _____ .	Consistent
6. Systems of ideas which are extrinsically invalid are "closed" and lose their intrinsic consistency when applied to another system or different phenomena. **No Response**	Consistent Invalid
7. A system of ideas which is externally invalid and consistent only with itself is a _____ system.	
8. A closed system is a group of ideas which are _____ and yet perhaps are _____ _____ .	Closed
9. Write the definition of a closed system.	Intrinsically Consistent Extrinsically Invalid
10. If you were to stop thinking now your mind would probably become a _____ _____ .	See Frame 1. (Review if your answer is not adequate.)
Sets 11. A simple example of a closed system is a *set*. A *set* is a well-defined collection of objects which share one or more common property. **No Response**	Closed System (It's good you're keeping with it!)
12. A well-defined collection of objects which share one or more common property is known as a _____ .	
13. Since oranges, lemons, tangerines, and limes share specific similarities, they all belong to the citrus fruit _____ .	Set

14. A set of well-defined objects may be expanded to contain several subsets. For example, an apple and a grape may be added to the citrus fruit set, thereby creating a new set including all fruits. **No Response**	Set
15. This diagram may clarify the overlapping of sets. **No Response** [[citrus—fruit set] set of all fruit]	
16. In the diagram of fruits, one ____________ overlaps another ____________.	
17. Since a set is a well-defined collection of objects which share common properties that contain intrinsic consistency, a set is an example of a c ____________ s ____________.	Set Set
18. Some numbers may represent a set since they are capable of sharing a common property. **No Response**	Closed System
19. For example, the following numbers: 154 257 653 share five tens as a common property. **No Response**	
20. Indicate which of the following rows of numbers share a common property as a set. **Check (X) Each Correct Row(s).** ____(A) 125 487 396 ____(B) 267 254 283 ____(C) 335 447 219	
21. Which of the following rows of symbols share a common property as a set? **Check Correct Row(s).** ____(A) ____(B) ____(C) ____(D) 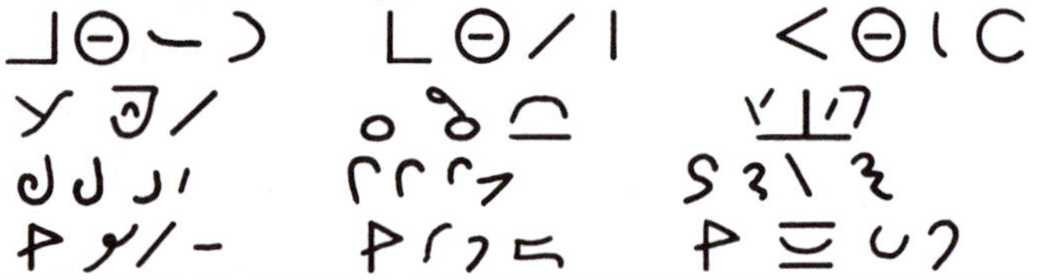	**(B) Two Hundreds is a Common Property**
22. A closed system represented as a collection of objects sharing one or more common properties is called a ____________.	**(A)** ⊖ **(D)** 
23. Define the term "set" and make up your own set of three or more symbols.	Set
24. The relationship between the arithmetic numbers 1 to 2 to 3 is always invariate in base ten. Also, 1 + 2 always equals 3. In this sense numbers represent a ____________ ____________.	**See Frame 11 (Review if Answer is Inadequate) Symbols Should Match Definition**

25. However, a problem arises when this simple arithmetic system is used extrinsically to quantify other areas, activities, or products. When this happens a transfer (from one closed system to another) must be made that may or may not be valid. **No Response**	Closed System
26. For instance, to state that "one apple plus one apple equals two apples" presents a *justifiable transfer* from one closed system to another. **No Response**	
27. The statement "one apple plus one kumquat equals two pieces of fruit" is also a *justifiable transfer*. **No Response**	
28. However, to state that "one apple plus one atom plus one universe equals three things" is stretching the transfer of a numerically closed system to a point where the transfer is perhaps extrinsically invalid.	
29. In going from one closed system to another when the two systems contain similar aspects or some similar relationship, then a _____ transfer is made.	
Language and Transfer 30. Another closed system that we use daily is language. For instance, English words may become a closed system when we step onto the shores of Arabia. English words have little meaning in the Arabic language. **No Response**	Justifiable or Valid
31. English words are not found in the Arabic language, because each language represents a _____ _____ .	
32. "Transfer" is the process of moving an object, symbol, or idea from one closed system to another yet retaining a similar meaning. The process of moving an object or idea from one closed system to another is called _____ .	Closed System
33. How much Arabic could one (versed only in English) learn with an Arabic dictionary if one knew nothing about Arabic symbols and meanings (that is, in a situation where transfer would exist between English and Arabic)?	Transfer
34. Since there are no similar symbols and meanings between English and Arabic, there would be no _____ of meaning.	None
35. Some languages have similar symbols (letters and words) as well as meanings in common and therefore allow for greater transfer. For example, English and French share approximately 46% cognates or words with similar spellings and meanings. **No Response**	Transfer

36.	Since English and French share 46% cognates, they have many common words which allow for some _____ .	
37.	There is no transfer of symbols and meanings between English and Arabic because each language represents a c _____ s _____ .	Transfer
38.	Transfer in languages is possible when similarities occur, such as, a common alphabet. Cognates can occur only when a common alphabet is used. Transfer in languages is possible when a common _____ is used.	Closed System
39.	When languages share a common alphabet, transfer is possible. English and Chinese however use very different letters or characters and thus allow no transfer. English and Chinese are (more, less) closed than English and French.	Alphabet
40.	Transfer is the process of moving an object, symbol, or idea from one _____ _____ to another.	More

Modes of Inquiry

41.	Another example of a closed system is represented by different "modes of inquiry." A mode of inquiry is a particular way of thinking about a subject or idea; it may represent a point of view. A particular mode of inquiry may represent another example of a _____ _____ .	Closed System (If incorrect, review from frame 32.)
42.	A particular way of thinking about a subject or idea or a definitive point of view generally represents a _____ _____ _____ .	Closed System
43.	Mode of inquiry represents a type of closed system when it represents a particular way of thinking which has intrinsic consistency. For example, assume that a particular religion has a consistent way of sequencing to explain the existence of God (god). **No Response**	Mode of Inquiry
44.	To explain the existence of God, this particular religion has a consistent _____ _____ _____ .	
45.	To explain the creation of man, advocates of evolution theory may have a different _____ _____ _____ than advocates of other points of view.	Mode of Inquiry or Point of View
46.	Modes of inquiry have their own internal logic independent of outside sources. Three common modes of inquiry might include the (1) "phenomenological," (2) "assumptive," and (3) "hypothetical." **No Response**	Mode of Inquiry (or words of similar meaning)

6

47. In the formulas for modes of inquiry, the slash sign "/" indicates "exclusive from," the three dotted sign "∴" means "therefore," while parenthesis "()" indicate a "tentative hypothesis." For example, fruit/meat suggests that fruit exists exclusive from meat; an egg ∴ chicken might mean the egg exists, therefore the chicken exists; and (given an effective umbrella) one will not get wet in the rain.

No Response

48. The sign "/" indicates _____ _____ , the sign "∴" indicates _____ , and the sign "()" symbolizes a

_____ _____ .

	Exclusive From
	Therefore
	Tentative Hypothesis

49. *Mode of Inquiry*   *Formula*

"Phenomenological"   A / B   C

"Assumptive"   A ∴ B   C

"Hypothetical"   (A) B   C ∴ A

If A is a belief which is held, the "Phenomenological" person might say that no empirical proof is necessary for the belief. The "Assumptive" person knows without doubt that A is so, and looks for proof of A. The "Hypothetical" person looks at the world, forms an hypothesis and based upon the evidence concludes A.

No Response

50. If A is a belief which is held, the "Phenomenological" person says that no *empirical* proof is necessary for the belief, the phenomenon itself constitutes its own reality.

Check (X) the "Phenomenological" Formula

_____1. A / B   C

_____2. A ∴ B   C

_____3. (A) B   C ∴ A

51. If A is a belief which is held, the "Assumptive" person knows without doubt that A is so, and looks continually for proof of A.

Check (X) the "Assumptive" Formula

_____1. (A) B   C ∴ A

_____2. A / B   C

_____3. A ∴ B   C

1. A / B   C

52. If A is a belief which is held, the "Hypothetical" person looks at the world, forms an hypothesis and based upon the evidence concludes A if indeed (A) is empirically verified.

Check the "Hypothetical" Formula

_____1. A / B   C

_____2. (A) B   C ∴ A

_____3. A ∴ B   C

3. A ∴ B   C

7

53. In explaining the existence of God fundamental Christians, agnostics, atheists, and scientists often argue_____ _____ _____.	2. (A) B C∴ A
54. The religionist who says "I know God exists" is generally speaking from the _____ mode of inquiry.	Modes of Inquiry
55. One may speak from the "phenomenological" mode of inquiry because one knows that God exists and perhaps no empirical proof of any kind will alter this belief. No Response	Phenomenological or Assumptive
56. "For my thoughts are not your thoughts, neither are your ways my ways, saith the Lord. For as the heavens are higher than the earth, so are my ways higher than your ways, and my thoughts higher than your thoughts." Isaiah 55: 8, 9. No Response	
57. The atheist who says, "I know that God does not exist," also may speak from the _____ mode(s) of inquiry.	
58. The person who says, "God exists, just look at the trees and the sunset and the universe," might be speaking from the _____ mode of inquiry.	Phenomenological or Assumptive
59. This person begins with a belief A and looks for proof of that belief. This person is combining _____ in God and _____ for that belief.	Assumptive
60. On the question of the empirical existence of God the "Hypothetical" or scientific mode of inquiry may lead to agnosticism as no definitive *empirical* proof of God's existence may be possible; however, the agnostic could look at certain relationships in the world which might demonstrate the existence of God: B and C and conclude perhaps A. No Response	Belief Proof
61. When the Christian says "I know God exists" and the scientist counters with "prove it" they are not arguing the existence of God as much as they are arguing _____ _____ _____.	
62. Three modes of inquiry representing closed systems in how people think are the_____ _____ and _____	Modes of Inquiry
63. Recall that a mode of inquiry is a particular way of thinking which has intrinsic consistency. Mode of inquiry is a closed system, just as a s____ is a closed system.	"Phenomenological" "Assumptive" "Hypothetical"
64. In the scientific mode of inquiry one seeks knowledge based on experimental methods. One seeks, but does not begin with "truth," only an operationally defined hypothesis (A). No Response	Set

65. From the scientific mode of inquiry one can only deal with the empirical world and measure that which is demonstrable. Additionally, should one rely on ones own subjective feelings to verify a scientific conclusion, one would be working simultaneously in more than one mode of inquiry. In such a case the extrinsic _____ is more questionable.	
66. The "Phenomenologists" might say, "I know that 'X' exists" while the experimenter might say, "I have some data to support that 'X' exists." These are examples of two different _____ of _____ .	Transfer or Validity
67. The statement "I know Mozart is a great composer, why just look at how many symphonies he wrote" is generally made from the _____ mode of inquiry.	Modes of Inquiry or Similar Words
68. A "Scientific" experimenter's mode of inquiry deals with empirical data that can be observed and measured. Place A Check (X) Beside the Item(s) Useable in "Scientific" Experimentation in Music: ____ A. Metronome ____ B. Soothsayer ____ C. Stroboconn ____ D. "Good" Feelings ____ E. Mental Phenomena ____ F. Objective Rating Scale ____ G. Oracle ____ H. "Bad Mood" ____ I. Edgar Cayce ____ J. Oscillator	"Assumptive"
69. Define "mode of inquiry" and list three (3) common modes.	A, C, F, and J
Closed Systems in Music 70. Some closed systems in music include: Pitch Rhythm Harmony Tempo Timbre Dynamics Notation Form No Response	Way of Thinking that has Intrinsic Consistency (or similar words). Phenomenological Assumptive Hypothetical (Review frame 41 if any difficulty.)
71. These closed systems in music may also overlap 	

72. Musical frequency is sound as measured in cycles per second (Hz). Since frequency (pitch) can be isolated from other musical elements, such as, rhythm, harmony, form, and timbre, and retain its intrinsic consistency and identity, it is a closed system. A closed system in music which is measured in cycles per second is _____.	
73. Rhythm is isolated in the example of a drum cadence with only slight reference made to other elements, such as, pitch, harmony, form and timbre. The isolated, predominant closed system in a drum cadence is _____ .	Frequency
74. Tone clusters exhibit elements of pitch, harmony, and timbre but generally have little reference to rhythm and form. Tone clusters exhibit the overlapping of three _____ of music.	Rhythm
75. The element of dynamics may overlap pitch, rhythm, harmony, timbre, or any combination of the above. As student crescendos a long tone of high "D" on the clarinet, he is overlapping dynamics with _____ and _____ .	Elements
76. The many different elements of music each represent _____ _____ . Seldom is a single musical element isolated, usually several elements _____ and are used simultaneously.	Pitch and Timbre
77. Some closed systems found on musical scores include title, composer, tempo indication, staff, clef, meter symbols, key signatures, notes, rests, and dynamics. No Response	Closed Systems Overlap
78. List eight closed systems represented in the following example: Flout 'em and Scout 'em Moderato T.L. Kuhn (♩ = 84) 1. 3. 5. 7. 2. 4. 6. 8.	
79. Explain why a meter signature such as $\frac{4}{4}$ could represent a closed system.	See Frame 77
80. Explain why the composer's name on the score is a closed system.	Use Definition of a Closed System

81. List ten "closed systems" that may or may not relate directly to each other that you see on this musical score.

Use Definition of a Closed System

82. List only the closed systems on a musical score that are necessary to "sound" or perform the music.

See Frame 77.

Staff, Clef, Key Signature, Notes and Rests

Good Job, You Have Completed the Program!

II _____

A Programmed Guide to Mill's Canons

1. John Stuart Mill, a philosopher of the nineteenth century, formulated five guidelines, or "canons," for systematically pinpointing the causes of events. The five Mill's Canons provide systematic methods for identifying the _____ of events.	
2. Identifying the causes of events, as in the five_____ _____, establishes a basis for experimentation.	Causes
3. The five Mill's Canons offer methods to identify_____* * *_____ and thereby _____* * *_____. (*** = More Than One Word Per Blank)	Mill's Canons
4. The rationale of Mill's Canons holds that if the cause of an event can be determined, an experimental design could be created for study of that event. Identifying the cause of an event precedes determining the experimental_____.	Causes of Events A Basis for Experimentation
5. Mill holds that the experimental design for an event cannot be completed without_____* * *_____.	Design
6. The importance of Mill's Canons to the beginning experimenter in music is that they provide a verbal rationale for designing an experiment. The music researcher with little experience in the scientific disciplines is offered a_____ _____ for experimental design by the Mill's Canons.	First Identifying the Cause of the Event
7. Mill's *Method of Agreement* proposes that if the circumstances leading up to a given event have in every case **Only One Common Factor**, that factor is probably the cause. Therefore, if in each occurrence of a given event, the circumstances preceding that event have only one common factor, the Method of _____ states that the common factor is probably the cause.	Verbal Rationale
8. A factor can be assumed to be the_____of an event if that factor is the_____ _____factor in the circumstances leading to that event.	Agreement
9. The sets SVT, RQS, OPS are three circumstances, with three factors each, leading to event B: SVT → B RQS → B OPS → B Notice that "S" is the _____ _____ factor in the circumstances leading to event B.	Cause Only Common

10. In the example in Frame #9 on the previous page: Applying Mill's Method of Agreement,_____ can be assumed to be the cause of event B because _____ * * * _____.	Only Common
11. In applying the Method of Agreement, which states * * * there is a possibility for error if one too quickly assumes that All other factors are dissimilar.	S Circumstances Leading Up to the Event Have Only One Common Factor
12. Mill's *Method of Differences* proposes that if two or more sets of circumstances are alike in every respect except for one factor and if a given event occurs only when that factor is present, the factor in question probably is the cause of that event. The Method of Differences is based on circumstances which are alike in every way with the exception of _____ _____.	If Circumstances Leading Up to a Given Event Have in Every Case Only One Common Factor, that Factor is the Cause
13. Referring to the Method of Differences, when two or more sets of circumstances are_____ in every respect except one, and that event occurs only when the one factor is present _* * *_ can be assumed to be the cause of the event.	One Factor
14. A commonly used experimental design uses carefully matched pairs of subjects; one member of each pair is assigned to the control group and the other member is assigned to the experimental group. If, after administering a treatment to the experimental group, the pair members are no longer identical, the cause of the change may be attributed to the treatment factor, the only factor not common to both groups. This illustrates Mill's Method of _____.	Alike The Factor in Question
15. In the circumstances preceding an event, only one common factor can be discerned. This common factor is assumed to be the cause of the event. This situation illustrates Mill's Method of_____.	Differences
16. A group of fifth grade students are divided randomly into two groups, one experimental and one control group. Both groups work assigned mathematical problems, but only the experimental group works in the presence of background music. This example is within the Method of Differences in that there are _____ _____ groups with _____ _____ unlike factor.	Agreement
17. In actual experimentation, a possible problem in attempting to hold all circumstances totally consistent except for the one factor under scrutiny, i.e., a problem in using the Method of_____, is that it is nearly impossible to make everything *exactly* the same.	Two Like Only One

18. Mill's *Joint Method* combines the first two methods. First, the one factor common to an occurrence is found (Method of Agreement), and second, the factor is withdrawn to determine if the phenomenon occurs only when the factor is present. The first step in the Joint Method is to find the _____ _____ .	Differences
19. Once a common factor has been found, that factor is _____ _____ to determine if the phenomenon occurs _____ when that factor is _____ .	Common Factor
20. A combination of the Method of Agreement and the Method of Differences results in Mill's _____ Method.	Withdrawn Only Present
21. All orchestras have conductors to direct the performance of the orchestra. If the conductor is withdrawn, will an evaluation show any difference in the performance of the orchestra? This example follows the Joint Method in that the conductor is a _____ _____ to orchestras and that he was _____ to evaluate the effect of this on the orchestra.	Joint
22. The first step of the Joint Method employs Mill's Method of _____ , which calls for isolating the _____ _____ from the preceding circumstances.	Common Factor Withdrawn
23. The second step of the Joint Method employs Mill's Method of _____ , to test whether, after withdrawing the _____ _____ , the event will ___* * *___ .	Agreement Common Factor
24. Mill's Canons offer methods to identify ____* * *____ and thereby establish ___ * * * ___ .	Differences Common Factor Fail to Recur
25. Thus far, we have discussed three of Mill's Canons. They are _____ * * * ___.	Causes of Events A Basis for Experimentation
26. Another of Mill's Canons, the *Method of Residues*, proposes that when the specific factors causing certain parts of a given phenomenon are known, the remaining parts of the phenomenon must be caused by the remaining factors. This method is concerned with the known and _____ factors of a given phenomenon.	Method of Agreement Method of Differences Joint Method
27. When the _____ factors causing certain parts of a given phenomenon are known, the remaining parts of the phenomenon must be caused by the _____ factors.	Unknown
28. A certain mouthpiece and practice routine are observed in exact detail among twenty horn players. However, all twenty players perform with different intonation patterns. This is an example of the Method of _____ .	Specific Remaining

29. The Method of Residues uses the process of _____ to try to find causes for a phenomenon.	Residues
30. Mill's *Method of Concomitant Variations* proposes that when two things consistently change or vary together, either the variations in one are caused by the variations in the other, or both are being affected by some common cause. This method is concerned with the consistent change of _____ factors.	Elimination
31. The word "concomitant" in the phrase "concomitant variation" means that of two factors, for example, _____ factors must vary _____.	Two
32. There are two ways in which things change or vary together: when _____ in one causes variation in the other, or when ___ * * * ___ effects both.	Both Consistently or Together
33. As a conductor of an orchestra changes his concert programming from popular classics to contemporary music, the size of the audience diminishes. This example follows the Method of Concomitant Variations in that two things, the programming and the size of the audience, ___ * * * ___.	Variation A Common Cause
34. When two factors consistently change together, one might be alerted to employ the Method of _____.	Vary Consistently Together
35. John Stuart Mill formulated _____ "canons" for determining the causes of particular events.	Concomitant Variation
36. Mill's Canons were devised by ___ * * * ___, a nineteenth century philosopher.	Five
37. Mill's Canons offer methods to identify ___ * * * ___ and thereby establish ___ * * * ___.	John Stuart Mill
38. The five Mill's Canons are titled: a. _____ b. _____ c. _____ d. _____ e. _____	The Causes of an Event A Basis for Experimentation
39. Two like groups of trumpet players are divided into an experimental group and a control group. The experimental group uses a specified mouthpiece and the control group uses their own mouthpieces. Which Mill's Canon describes this event?	a. Agreement b. Differences c. Joint d. Residues e. Concomitant Variations

40. A study was made of twenty persons that have perfect pitch. All twenty were found to have an I.Q. of 120 or more. This was the only common factor in the group and was assumed to be the cause of their having perfect pitch. Which Mill's Canon describes this event? — Method of Differences

41. Brass players have found that as room temperature rises, they tend to play sharp. Which Mill's Canon describes this event? — Method of Agreement

42. Five Clarinet players were assessed to have played with a good tone. It was found that the only common factor that they shared was the use of the same brand of reed. They were given a different brand of reed and their tone was again evaluated. Which Mill's Canon describes this event? — Method of Concomitant Variations

43. It is known that listening to music is an aural experience, but the extent of the physiological effects of music is not fully understood. Which Mill's Canon describes this event? — Joint Method

Method of Residues

III

A Programmed Guide to Selected Research Designs and Statistical Tests

SELECTED RESEARCH DESIGNS AND STATISTICAL TESTS

Hypothesis of No Difference (two-tail) Hypothesis of Predictable Difference (one-tail)
Area of rejection when p = .05

	One-Sample			Two-Sample				Multiple-Sample			
				Equivalent		Independent		Equivalent		Independent	
DESIGNS	*Post-test only*	*Post-test only*	*Pre-test-Post-test*	*Post-test only*	*Pre-test-Post-test*	*Post-test only*	*Pre-test-Post-test*	*Post-test only*	*Pre-test-Post-test*	*Pre-test-Post-test*	*Pre-test-Post-test*
									MO_1XO_2 MO_1 O_2		O_1XO_3 O_1 O_3
					M $\begin{matrix}XO \\ O\end{matrix}$				XO	$O_1X_1O_2$	XO_1
	XO	X_1X_2O	O_1XO_2	M $\begin{matrix}XO \\ O\end{matrix}$	M $\begin{matrix}O_1XO_2 \\ O_1\ O_2\end{matrix}$	XO O	$\begin{matrix}O_1XO_2 \\ O_1\ O_2\end{matrix}$	M $\begin{matrix}XO \\ O\end{matrix}$	M $\begin{matrix}XO_1 \\ O_1\end{matrix}$	$O_1X_2O_2$ $O_1\ O_2$	O_1

RESEARCH	*Classification or ranking*	*Subjects as own control*	*Post-test only*	*Pre-test-Post-test*		*Post-test only*	*Pre-test-Post-test*	*Matching by Counterbalance*	*Temporal.*	*Counterbalance*	*Temporal*
								$X_1OX_2OX_3OX_4O$	$MO_1X_1O_2X_2O_3X_3O_4$	$X_1OX_2OX_3OX_4O$	$O_1X\ O_2O_3O_4$
								$X_2OX_3OX_4OX_1O$	$MO_1\ O_2X_3O_3X_4O_4$	$X_2OX_3OX_4OX_1O$	$O_1O_2X\ O_3O_4$
	$O_1O_2O_3O_4O_5$		M $\begin{matrix}X_1O \\ X_2O\end{matrix}$	O_1M	$\begin{matrix}XO_2 \\ O_2\end{matrix}$	$\begin{matrix}X_1O \\ X_2O\end{matrix}$	O_1 $\begin{matrix}XO_2 \\ O_2\end{matrix}$	$X_3OX_4OX_1OX_2O$	$MO_1\ \ O_2\ \ O_3X_3O_4$	$X_3OX_4OX_1OX_2O$	$O_1O_2O_3X\ O_4$
	etc.	$O_1XO_2XO_3$						$X_4OX_1OX_2OX_3O$	$MO_1\ \ O_2\ \ O_3\ \ O_4$	$X_4OX_1OX_2OX_3O$	$O_1O_2O_3O_4\ \ O_5$

| **NOMINAL MEASUREMENT** | χ^2 *One-Sample Test.* Goodness of fit for testing expected vs. observed frequencies (e.g., preferences among defined categories on questionnaire, performance rating scale, etc.). *Binomial Test.* Goodness of fit for testing two discrete categories (e.g., flat-sharp, loud-soft, correct-incorrect). | *McNemar Test for Significance of Changes.* Used when the two categories are not related in measurement levels i.e., when one or both categories achieve only nominal level (e.g., comparing musical judgments good-bad with rank order judgments). Excellent when subject acts as own control. | *Fisher Exact Probability Test.* Used with small N to test differences between samples on basis of central tendency in a 2×2 table. χ^2 *Test for Independent Samples.* Used to test differences between samples on basis of *any* discrete differences between the two populations. | | | | | *Cochran Q Test.* Used to test whether three or more matched sets differ significantly among themselves on the basis of dichotomous data (e.g., yes-no, flat-sharp, correct-incorrect). Matching may be between different subjects or on different observations for each subject. | | χ^2 *Test for Multiple Independent Samples.* Used to test significant differences among samples. | |

| **ORDINAL MEASUREMENT** | *Kolmogorov-Smirnov One-Sample Test.* Goodness of fit for testing ranked data (e.g., pre- vs. post-test measures, questionnaire, performance rating scale). Preferred to χ^2 if sample is small. | *Wilcoxon Matched Pairs.* Used when measurements achieve ordinal level both *between* and *within* pairs. *Sign test.* Used when ordinal measurements achieved only within pairs. | *Mann-Whitney U.* Used to test differences in samples on basis of central tendency. Most powerful alternate to the parametric t test. *Kolmogorov-Smirnov Two-Sample Test.* Used to test significance between samples on basis of *any* differences between populations (two-tail) or central tendency (one-tail). | | | | | *Friedman Two-Way Analysis of Variance.* Used to test whether three or more matched sets differ significantly among themselves on basis of mean ranks for each set. | | *Kruskal-Wallis One-Way Analysis of Variance.* Used to test significant differences among samples on basis of ranks. This test is always preferred to χ^2 if data qualify. | |

| **INTERVAL OR RATIO MEASUREMENT** | *t Test.* Used to test significance between the sample mean and theoretical distribution or pre- and post-test differences. | *t Test.* Used to test significance between related sample means or means of different scores. *Walsh Test.* Used to test significance between samples of ranked differences when N is less than 15. | *t Test.* Used to test significance between independent sample means. *Randomization Test for Two Independent Samples.* Used to test significance between independent sample means. Should be used with small N. | | | | | *Analysis of Variance.* Used to test whether three or more matched samples differ significantly among themselves on basis of variance between sample means. | | *Analysis of Variance.* Used to test whether three or more independent samples differ significantly on basis of variance between sample means. | |

X = Experimental Variable (treatments)
O = Observation (measurements)
M = Matching on basis of known attributes or pre-test by pairs of subjects, groups, or by using each subject as own control

From *Experimental Research in Music* by Madsen and Madsen, p. 84. (1970) Prentice-Hall, Inc. Used by permission of the authors and publishers.

INTRODUCTION

1. The chart on page 84 of *Experimental Research in Music* is entitled "Selected Research Designs and Statistical Tests." It was organized for the beginning researcher. Its main purpose is to demonstrate how statistical tests are structured to *coincide* with

   the research_____of a study.

2. In order to utilize the chart, there are several discriminations about the research design that must be made. When the research design has been fully determined, the chart may be used to select an appropriate, coinciding _____ _____.	Design
3. This program is organized to help you utilize the chart effectively. Several theoretical studies will be used to facilitate demonstration of the chart.	Statistical Test

Determining Sample Size and Relationships

4. **Look at the Chart.** It shows that the first discrimination to be made about our theoretical study is the number of *samples* dealt with. A **Sample** is a collection of observations drawn from some defined **Population.** Let us say our theoretical study concerns observations of brass instrument mouthpieces. We might define the **population** of this study as all brass instrument mouthpieces ever utilized or invented. Obviously, it would be impossible to find *every* brass instrument mouthpiece in order to observe it. But, representative pieces or_____could be drawn from the population and observed.	
5. In this study, *all* brass instrument mouthpieces would represent the_____.	Samples
6. Those brass instrument mouthpieces actually *observed* represent the_____in this study.	Population
7. Experiments may generally be classified in one of three groups: (1) the **One-sample Method,** (2) the **Two-sample Method,** and (3) **The Multiple-sample Method.**	Sample
8. In the **One-sample Method,** one sample is drawn from a _____.	
9. When the one sample has been *observed,* it may then be compared statistically with what might be *expected* of such a sample. Such statistical tests are known as "goodness of fit" tests. They compare how well data fits, on the basis of observed vs._____ frequencies.	Population
10. In order to achieve some form of *control* in the _____ -Sample Method, more than one observation may be taken. This is usually done before (pre) and after (post) any experimental manipulations. Comparisons are then made on the basis of change in individual subjects. This technique utilizes the subject as his own _____.	Expected

11. "Goodness of fit" statistical tests and use of subjects as their own control are common factors in the _____ _____ Method.	One Control
12. In the **Two-sample Method**, two samples are drawn from the population. The samples are treated differently and the differences between samples compared statistically. By design, the *relationship* between the two samples may be either **Equivalent** or **Independent**. When the two samples are *matched* on the basis of known attributes or pretest, the relationship is _____.	One-Sample
13. If a research design utilizes two equivalent samples, this would indicate that pairs of subjects or groups have been equated or _____.	Equivalent
14. Another relationship exists if no attempt has been made to make the two samples similar. Two unmatched samples are said to be _____.	Matched
15. If a research design utilizes two independent samples, this would indicate that the samples have *not* been _____.	Independent
16. Whether the sample relationship is equivalent or independent is inherent in the research _____ of the study.	Matched
17. Most often, control in the **Two-sample Method** is gained through the use of pre- and posttesting. The two samples (which have been manipulated differently) are compared on the amount of change noted between the _____ and _____ tests. However, sometimes a posttest only is used.	Design
18. In the **Multiple-sample Method**, three or more samples are drawn from the population. These samples are treated differently, and differences between samples compared. Like the **Two-sample Method**, the relationship between the samples may be either _____ or _____.	Pre Post
19. If a study is designed with more than one sample, an important discrimination to be made is the _____ between the samples.	Equivalent Independent
<div align="center">DETERMINING THE SEQUENCE OF TREATMENTS AND MEASUREMENTS</div>	
20. The number and relationship of samples in our theoretical study has been determined. It is now important to know what sequence of **Treatments** and **Measurements** was utilized in the design. Those observations which comprise the data and measure some aspect of the sample are the _____.	Relationship

21. The symbol O is used to indicate an *observation* or _____ taken on some aspect of the sample.	Measurements
22. A pre- or posttest is an example of a measurement or_____ taken on some aspect of the sample.	Measurement
23. Data are comprised of _____ or _____ taken on some aspect of a sample.	Observation
24. The symbol used for an observation or measurement is _____.	Observations Measurements
25. Those experimental variables manipulated at the demand of the experimenter and used to treat samples differently are called _____.	0
26. The symbol used to indicate treatment given to a sample is X. An X may be used to represent a new instruction, extra reinforcement, or special attention given to one sample. These experimental variables are called _____.	Treatments
27. The symbol used to indicate treatments manipulated by the experimenter is _____.	Treatments
28. Subscripts are used with both the symbols O and X to indicate *order* when more than one observation or treatment is used. For instance, a pretest would be 1 or O_1. A posttest would be observation 2 or _____.	X
29. Samples, whose relationship is equivalent, have been equated, or _____.	O_2
30. The symbol M is used to indicate matching of samples. A sample given a pretest and then matched would be represented by _____.	Matched
31. Two examples are given for utilizing symbols and subscripts in determining the sequence of treatments and measurements: a. a one-sample study using one treatment followed by a measurement (posttest). $$\underline{XO}$$ b. a two-sample study, matched on the basis of pretest, one treatment given to one group, both groups posttested. $$O_1 M \quad \begin{array}{c} XO_2 \\ \hline O_2 \end{array}$$ Determine if the following example is correct or incorrect. $$O_1 \quad \begin{array}{c} X_1 O_2 \\ X_2 O_2 \\ X_3 O_2 \\ X_4 O_2 \\ \hline O_2 \end{array}$$	O M

This is an example of a multiple-sample study using five independent samples with pre- and posttesting and four different treatments.

Correct or Incorrect?

32.	Now, Write symbols for the following study: three independent samples with pre- and posttest and one treatment given to Group 1, one treatment given to Group 2, and no treatments given to Group 3.	Correct

DETERMINING LEVEL OF MEASUREMENT

33.	For our theoretical study, the number and relationships of samples and sequence of treatments and measurements have now been determined. The next discrimination involves the level of measurement of the data. Determining the level of measurement is to some extent a value judgment. There are, however, basic rules to help shape your decision. There are four general types of measurement scales used in experimentation: (1) nominal, (2) ordinal, (3) interval, (4) ratio. The four scales above are given in order of weakest (general) to strongest (specific) levels of_____ .	X_1 O_2 O_1 X_2 O_2 O_2
34.	The *nominal* or "naming" scale is used solely for classification. It is the weakest and most_____level of measurement.	Measurement
35.	Some examples of the nominal scale are: flat-sharp; good-bad; yes-no; + or −. This most general level of measurement allows only comparisons between groups of **Equality** and **Differences**. No comparisons can be made *within groups* at the _____ level.	General
36.	The next highest level of measurement is the ordinal level. Like the nominal scale, the ordinal scale can also make the general comparisons of_____ and_____ .	Nominal
37.	The strength of the ordinal scale lies in its ability to allow comparisons of members within groups by ordering or *ranking* those members. Statements such as greater than or less than may be made about the individual members, but *how much* greater or less than may *not* be made. A preference scale of 1-7; grades of A,B,C; *total* scores on *tests* consisting of points assigned to many separate items; or chair assignments in a band on the basis of tryouts are all examples of the_____ level of measurement.	Equality Differences
38.	The above examples are ordinal scales because they allow comparisons of individuals within groups by_____those individuals.	Ordinal
39.	At the ordinal level, an experimenter may say that one individual did better than other individuals. He may not say _____better.	Ranking (or ordering)

40. At this level, value judgments become apparent in determining levels of measurement. For instance, some people believe IQ scores to be true measures of intelligence and relegate them to a high level of measurement. If this is done, one can make statements about how much smarter a child with an IQ of "103" is than a child with an IQ of "100." If you believe IQ scores to reflect only ability to answer questions on intelligence tests, you would relegate IQ scores to a _____ level of measurement.	How Much
41. For example, if you believe that IQ tests represent ordinal level of measurement, then you might say that a child with an IQ of "103" performed better in answering questions than did a child with an IQ of "100." You would not say _____ _____ better one child did than another.	Lower
42. Only Nonparametric statistics are appropriate for the first two levels of measurement; therefore, Nonparametric statistics can be used with either _____ or _____ levels of measurement.	How Much
43. Place an N beside measurements at the nominal level and an O beside measurements at the ordinal level. _____a. score of 95 on history test _____b. retarded-normal _____c. rhythm, melody, harmony _____d. first chair Flute at all-state band	Nominal Ordinal
44. The *interval* scale is stronger than both the _____ and _____ scales.	(a) O (b) N (c) N (d) O
45. The interval scale permits comparisons of equality and _____.	Nominal Ordinal
46. It also permits comparisons of greater-than and less-than as does the _____ level of measurement.	Differences
47. The strength of interval measurement lies in its ability to assess *intervallic* comparisons. These comparisons are possible since <u>Distances</u> between points on this scale are <u>Known</u>. Common examples of interval measurement are the metronome, calendar, and thermometer. These are scales permitting _____ comparisons.	Ordinal
48. Intervallic comparisons are made on the basis of _____ _____ between scale points.	Intervallic
49. The interval level is the first level at which **Parametric** statistics are appropriately used. At the nominal and ordinal levels, only _____ statistics are used.	Known Distances

50. The levels of measurement in order from weakest to strongest thus far discussed are: (1)_____ , (2)_____ , and (3)_____ .	Nonparametric
51. The strongest, or most specific, level of measurement is the *ratio* scale. It permits measurements of _____ and differences.	(1) Nominal (2) Ordinal (3) Interval
52. The ratio level also permits greater-than/less-than comparisons and intervallic comparisons. Its strength lies in the fact that not only does it have known distances between points, but also an **Absolute Zero** point. Values may be doubled, tripled, etc., because of this **Absolute Zero** point in _____ level of measurement.	Equality
53. Most ratio levels are achieved through the use of sophisticated apparati such as electric timers, voice spectrographs, etc. Statistical tests appropriate at the ratio and interval levels of measurement are _____ .	Ratio
54. The levels of measurement in order from weakest to strongest are: (1)_____ , (2)_____ , (3)_____ , and (4)_____ .	Parametric
55. Place an *N* beside measurements at the nominal level, an *O* beside those at the ordinal level, an *I* for those at interval and an *R* for Ratio: ____a. running the mile in 3.546 min. by stopwatch ____b. beautiful-ugly ____c. on-task, off-task ____d. Ph.D. dissertation 7″ thick by ruler ____e. a rank ordering of the world's greatest pianists	(1) Nominal (2) Ordinal (3) Interval (4) Ratio

FINDING AN APPROPRIATE STATISTICAL TEST

56. Once the number and relationship of samples and level of measurement of the data have been determined, we are ready to locate an appropriate statistical test for our theoretical study. **Look at the Chart.** It is designed with number and relationship of samples arranged in columns. Levels of measurement are arranged in rows. At the point where the appropriate column and row intersect are suggested statistical tests which would fit the design of our theoretical study. For example, a study utilizing two equivalent samples with data measured at the nominal level is matched with the "McNemar Test for Significance of Changes." $M\begin{pmatrix} X_1 O \\ X_2 O \end{pmatrix}$ Those tests suggested at the nominal and ordinal levels of measurement are _____ statistical tests.	(a) R (b) N (c) N (d) I or R (e) O

57. Those tests suggested at the interval and ratio level of measurement are _____ statistical tests.	Nonparametric
58. Find an appropriate statistical test for a study utilizing two independent samples with data at the ordinal level. This test would be the _____ or _____ . $\left(O_1 \begin{array}{c} XO_2 \\ O_2 \end{array} \right)$	Parametric
59. The test chosen is a _____ statistical test.	Mann-Whitney U or Kolmogorov—Smirnoff
60. When more than one statistical test is suggested, the choice should be based on exactly what effect the study deals with. Siegel's *Nonparametric Statistics* and Campbell & Stanley's *Experimental and Quasi-Experimental Designs for Research* are suggested readings to aid in making this decision. The object of your decision is to make the statistical test coincide as closely as possible with the research _____ of the study.	Nonparametric
WRITING THE HYPOTHESIS	
61. Research in the behavioral sciences is usually conducted to ascertain the acceptability of hypotheses. *Hypotheses* are statements formulated from theories of behavior. Data are collected about a stated _____ .	Design
62. Data help us determine whether the stated hypothesis should be retained, revised, or rejected. Therefore, research is a continuous decision-making procedure which *shapes* a theory. The first step in this decision-making process is stating an _____ .	Hypothesis
63. A series of data concerning hypotheses help shape _____ .	Hypothesis
64. A Research Hypothesis predicts the outcome of an experiment on the basis of the theory under test. The hypothesis to be *statistically* tested is the **Null Hypothesis**. It is referred to as null because it predicts ___ differences between samples being observed.	Theories
65. The Null Hypothesis is formulated for the express purpose of being *rejected* via the statistical test. It can be proved that something is not true or two things are not alike by logic. One only has to find one fault or difference to prove the case. Logically, one can never *prove* truth or likeness. There are an infinite number of variables to be compared before a decision can be made that something is true (or two things are alike). Therefore, an hypothesis to be tested statistically is usually stated in the _____ form.	No
66. Stating the hypothesis in a null form is a procedure based on ___.	Null

67.	The Null Hypothesis is always a statement of no_____ between samples.	Logic
68.	A Null Hypothesis is written for the express purpose of being _____ via the statistical test.	Differences
69.	In addition to stating a Null Hypothesis, the researcher usually formulates an **Alternative Hypothesis**. If the Null Hypothesis is rejected, the other, or_____, hypothesis may be accepted.	Rejected
70.	Acceptance of an alternative hypothesis lends support to the _____ being shaped.	Alternative
71.	When writing an hypothesis, there are two factors that should always be included: a. the expected *relation* of the *sample* to the *population* defined, and b. the expected *effect* of the *variable* in question. A Null Hypothesis is an hypothesis of no_____.	Theory
72.	If the study under question involves the amount of time taken by two groups of orchestra members to sight-read a violin score, the Null Hypothesis (H_o) would be stated: H_o: The two *groups are* from the *same population* and there will be *no difference* in the mean* amount of time taken to sight-read the violin score. (*Mean is used so the two groups can be compared as whole entities. Scores are averaged for each group and means compared.) The above hypothesis contains the two important factors in hypothesis writing: a. the expected relation of the sample to the_____, and b. the expected effect of the_____ in question.	Differences
73.	An alternative hypothesis (H_1) may either predict a difference in *general* or predict a difference in a *specified direction*. An alternative hypothesis predicting a *specified direction* of difference is a **One-tailed** hypothesis. An alternative hypothesis predicting a *general* difference is a **Two-** _____ hypothesis.	Population Variable
74.	A possible alternative hypothesis for the study mentioned above is: H_1: The two *groups* are *not* from the *same population* and there *will be a* difference in the mean amount of time taken by each group to sight-read the violin score. This is a _____ -tailed alternative hypothesis.	Tailed

75.	The above hypothesis predicts only a _____ difference between groups.	Two
76.	This hypothesis contains the two important factors in hypothesis writing: a. the expected relation of the samples to the population, and b. _____.	General
77.	Another alternative hypothesis which might be written for the same study is: H_1: The two *groups* are *not* from the *same* population and the group receiving the Super-Duper Method of Sight Reading will require less mean time to sight read the violin score than will the group receiving no instruction. This is a _____-tailed alternative hypothesis.	The Expected Effect of the Variable in Question
78.	It predicts a specified _____ of difference between the two groups.	One
79.	The above hypothesis contains the two important factors in hypothesis writing: a. the expected relation of _____ _____, and b. the expected effect of _____ _____.	Direction
80.	Write a Null Hypothesis for the following study. The question being studied concerns the musical aptitude of junior music majors as opposed to School of Music faculty. The test utilized is the "Gordon Music Ability Profile" (MAP). _____ _____ _____	(a) The Sample to the Population (b) The Variable in Question
81.	Write a two-tailed alternative hypothesis for the above study. _____ _____ _____ _____	H_o: The Two Groups Are from the Same Population and There Will Be No Difference Between the Mean M.A.P. Scores of Junior Music Majors and the Music Faculty.
82.	Write a one-tailed alternative hypothesis for the above study. _____ _____ _____ _____	H_1: The Two Groups Are Not from the Same Population and There Will Be a Difference Between the Mean M.A.P. Scores of Junior Music Majors and Music Faculty

UNDERSTANDING ONE- AND TWO-TAILED HYPOTHESES	H_1 : The Two Groups Are Not from the Same Population and the Mean Score of Junior Music Majors Will Be Higher (or Lower, Depending on Bias) than that of the School of Music Faculty
83. There are two possible ways in which an alternative hypothesis may be written. An alternative hypothesis predicting a *general* difference between samples is a _____-tailed hypothesis.	
84. An hypothesis predicting a specified direction of difference between samples is a _____-tailed hypothesis.	Two
85. The "One" and "Two-tailed" terms refer directly to the *region of rejection* under a normal curve. If all possible scores from the population of an experimental measurement were graphed, it is generally assumed they would form a "normal curve" as shown below: This graph shows the bulk of scores in the middle, and very low or very high scores in ends or _____ of the curves.	One
86. If our theoretical study is trying to demonstrate a *difference* between two groups. We would like this difference to be statistically *significant*. In order to be significant, the number derived as the difference must be so unusual as to have a very low probability of having occurred by chance alone instead of as a result of our experimental manipulations. The curve shows us that those scores with lowest frequencies, or probabilities, fall at the _____ of the curve.	Tails
87. A level is set within which a score must fall to be statistically *significant*. If we set .05 as this level, those scores with a probability of .05 occur at the _____.	Tails
88. This area at the tails of the curve set aside by the selected significance level is called the *region of rejection*. If the difference between samples falls in this area, the score is statistically _____.	Tails
89. A statistically significant score allows the null hypothesis to be _____.	Significant
90. If an alternative hypothesis predicts a general direction of difference, the significant scores could occur in either of _____ tails.	Rejected

91.	Group A could be greater than Group B and a significant score would occur in the + tail. Group A could be less than Group B and a significant score would occur in the − tail. A score is considered significant when it falls in the region of _____ .	Two
92.	An alternative hypothesis predicting a general difference between samples, then, equally divides its region of rejection into both tails of the normal curve and is called a _____ - _____ hypothesis.	Rejection
93.	An alternative hypothesis of specified direction of difference would state that Group A *will be greater* than Group B. With a significance level of .05, the statistically significant scores would *all* occur in the + tail of the curve. This is a _____ - _____ hypothesis.	Two-tailed
94.	If the alternative hypothesis was stated Group A *will be less* than Group B, the significant scores would *all* occur in the _____ tail of the curve.	One-tailed
95.	How does the researcher decide whether to use a one-tailed or two-tailed alternative hypothesis? *Most researchers generally conduct two-tailed alternative hypotheses*, though they are not quite so powerful as a one-tailed alternative hypothesis. The reason for this, is that two-tailed alternative hypotheses can *always* be tested, no matter what the outcome of the data. A one-tailed alternative hypothesis would be done only if the researcher was convinced that the data could *never* occur in a direction opposite from the one predicted. This is difficult, since experience shows that data acquired is seldom exactly what was expected. If you state an alternative hypothesis predicting Group A will be greater than Group B, and the data reveals that Group B (in this particular case) was greater than Group A—you are stuck. There are no statistical tests that can possibly be applied to this situation. There are also no statements or inferences that can be made about the study, population, or sample. To avoid this situation, most researchers conduct _____ - _____ alternative hypotheses.	—or Minus

CHOOSING THE SIGNIFICANCE LEVEL

96. Significance level is the probability of *mistakenly* rejecting the null hypothesis—i.e , rejecting the null hypothesis *by chance alone* instead of as a result of experimental manipulation. The symbol for significance level is α. This symbol is the Greek letter *alpha*. Many times you will hear significance referred to as alpha level. The significance level determines the region of _____.	Two-tailed
97. The region of rejection is the area under the normal curve where a difference score might occur that is statistically _____.	Rejection
98. A significant score allows rejection of the _____ hypothesis.	Significant
99. Choosing a significance level is rather arbitrary. There is nothing magical about .05 or .01— .04 or .02 would do just as well. Tradition has made .05 and .01 the most frequent _____ _____ chosen.	Null
100. Write the symbol for significance level: _____	Significance Levels
101. In choosing a significance level, the decision boils down to — how *certain* do you want to be that your findings are not due *to chance alone*? If you choose α = .05, you are 95% sure that your findings did not occur _____ _____ _____.	α
102. Some people feel comfortable making statements about their findings while being sure those findings did not occur by chance alone *90% of the time*. Those people have set α = _____.	By Chance Alone
103. α is the Greek letter _____.	.10
104. Some people refuse to attribute any relevance to research with an α greater than .001. These people are _____ % sure their findings did not occur by chance alone.	Alpha
105. "Truth is not established, it is approximated." The _____	99.9
	End

IV _____

A Programmed Guide to Basic Statistics *

[handwritten: MEAN & SD]

[handwritten: TRANSFER INFORMATION FROM INTO LARGER POPULATION]

DESCRIPTIVE AND INFERENTIAL STATISTICS

[handwritten: T-TEST]

Descriptive statistics describe certain characteristics about sets of data in concise, mathematical form. With just a few numbers one can describe how a group as a whole is performing (mean), how much variability there is within a group (variance), and how much relationship (correlation) exists between two groups. The relative position of a student within a certain group (Z score or percentiles) and predictions about that student's score on some other variable (regression) may also be described.

Another primary use of statistics is to make inferences about some large group or groups on the basis of information obtained from some smaller group or subset of the larger group. In inferential statistics the primary goal is often to determine some characteristic or characteristics of a large group or population. In descriptive statistics the concern is with relatively small groups that could be measured, and thus easily described. But in working with large groups or populations it is nearly always impossible to measure each and every case (subject) in order to be able to describe the group. In this case, only a few of the cases (a sample) from the total population are measured. This technique is called sampling.

SAMPLING

[handwritten: HAPHAZARD VS. RANDOM]

Sampling means taking a part from a whole. Since some characteristic of an entire population cannot be measured directly, a subset or sample from the larger population is selected and measured. It is then inferred that the measured characteristics of the sample accurately reflect the "real" characteristics of the population.

In order to be able to assume logically such an inference, one must try to make certain that the sample really "looks like" the population from which it came; that is, it must be representative of the larger population. This situation is accomplished by taking a random sample.

WHAT IS RANDOM?

Randomness means that every subset (sample) of size N from a population has an equal and independent chance of being selected for the sample.

A random sample taken from a population gives the best assurance possible that it will look like the population from which it comes. The only way to get a more representative sample would be to know what the population looked like in advance and select the sample in such a manner that its characteristics matched the population's characteristics exactly. But this is not the case very often. When a sample is drawn which is not representative of the population as a whole it is said to be biased.

HYPOTHESIS TESTING

An hypothesis is considered either true or false. A researcher's difficulty is that he can never be certain, even after he has tested the hypothesis, which it is. Thus, in analyzing the results of an experiment, there is always a risk of making one of two possible errors.

_____

*See: Glossary of Statistical Symbols (pp. 117).
    Basic Mathematical Procedures (pp. 118).
    Use of a Burroughs Calculator (p. 120) before beginning.
These will be helpful in completing the following two programs.

Suppose the experimenter rejects the null hypothesis and decides there is a difference. Possibly he is wrong: there may be no difference. On the other hand, suppose he fails to reject the null hypothesis. Again he may be wrong: there may actually be a difference which he failed to detect.

The logic of tests on statistical hypotheses is as follows: one assumes that the hypothesis one desires to test is true. Then he examines the consequences of this assumption in terms of a sampling distribution which depends upon the truth of this hypothesis. If as determined from the sampling distribution, observed data have a relatively high probability of occurring, then the decision is made that the data do not contradict the hypothesis. On the other hand, if the probability of an observed set of data is relatively low when the hypothesis is true, the decision is that the data tend to contradict the hypothesis. Frequently the hypothesis that is tested is stated in such a way that, when the data tend to contradict it, the experimenter is actually demonstrating what it is that he is trying to establish. In such cases the experimenter is interested in being able to reject or nullify the hypothesis being tested; in such a case, the name of the hypothesis under test is the null hypothesis.

The level of significance of a statistical test defines the probability level that is to be considered too low to warrant support of the null hypothesis being tested. If the probability of the occurrence of observed data (when the null hypothesis being tested is true) is smaller than the level of significance, then the data are said to contradict the null hypothesis being tested, and a decision is made to reject this hypothesis.

The null hypothesis being tested is designated by the symbol H_0.

The set of hypotheses that remain tenable when H_0 is rejected are called the alternative hypotheses and are designated by the symbols H_1, H_2, etc.

TWO TYPES OF ERRORS

The decision rules in a statistical test are with respect to the rejection or nonrejection of H_0. If the decision rules reject H_0 when in fact it is true, the rules lead to an erroneous decision. The level of significance sets an upper bound on the probability of making a decision to reject H_0 when in fact H_0 is true. This kind of erroneous decision is known as a Type I error; the probability of making a Type I error is controlled by the level of significance. Type I error is generally represented by alpha (α).

A Type II error occurs when the decision is to fail to reject the null hypothesis (accept H_0) when, in fact, some alternative hypothesis is true.

The potential magnitude of a Type II error depends in part upon the level of significance, in part upon which one of the possible alternative hypotheses is actually true, the size of the sample, and the size of the difference between groups (effect size) one wishes to detect. Type II error is generally represented by beta (β).

In the following summary table, rejection of H_0 is regarded as being equivalent to accepting H_1 and nonrejection of H_0 equivalent to not accepting H_1. The possibility of a Type I error exists only when the decision is to reject H_0; the possibility of a Type II error exists only when the decision is not to reject H_0.

Decision	Actual Situation	
	No Difference Among Groups	True Difference Among Groups
Reject H_0	Type I error	No error
Do not Reject H_0	No error	Type II error

TYPE I ERRORS

Remember that a Type I error is controlled by the level of significance. Thus, in the long run, during the course of a great many experiments, an investigator who is employing the .05 level of significance will be in error in 5% of the hypotheses he rejects. Naturally one would like to make the probability of a Type I error as low as possible. However, this desire is restricted by the need for rejecting the hypothesis when it is false. Suppose the level of significance is set at zero so that there is no statistical probability of an error of Type I. If this is done, however, there is no possibility of rejecting the hypothesis even when it is false.

TYPE II ERRORS

Declaring a hypothesis false might imply that one has some idea of what alternative situations exist. For example, in testing the hypothesis that the mean of a population = 5, possible alternative hypotheses might be that the true mean = 6, 3, 5.1, etc. In fact, alternatives might include any number except 5. If it happens that the true mean = 6, then there is a certain probability of rejecting the null hypothesis that it = 5. If the true mean = 3, then there is some other probability of rejecting the hypothesis that it is 5. This probability of rejecting the null hypothesis is called the power of the test.

POWER   *SAMPLE SIZE counts for Power*

Power $(1-\beta)$ depends upon which alternative hypothesis is actually true and in practice one does not know which alternative is true and is interested in the power of the test for several possible alternative hypotheses. If the null hypothesis is not true, then one would like the chance of rejecting it to be as large as possible and thus would like the power to be large. In general, reducing the level of significance increases the power of the test.

For a fixed level of significance, power is increased as sample size is increased. Sample size should be made as large as feasible to assure good power. If a sample size is small because of the nature of the study then the level of significance should not be very small. Since both low level of significance and small sample size contribute to a reduction in power, their combination is not desirable.

The use which is to be made of the information gained from an investigation plays a part in the selection of a level of significance. If the purpose of the study is to test a medicine for its potential power to kill the patient, an alpha level of .01 or .001 would be chosen. That is, one wants to be very sure that the medicine does not harm people.

On the other hand, if the purpose of the study is to choose some remedial action or a teaching method, the investigator would not wish to reject a method which may be helpful, even if the evidence in favor of the method is slight. Under such circumstances, the investigator would probably adopt the .05, .06, .10, or even .20 level of significance.

In most cases a two-tailed test should be performed. Only in a case where there is no logical possibility of the results coming out in the opposite direction should the test be one-tailed.

CONTINUOUS AND DISCRETE

Data occurs in one of two forms, continuous or discrete. If a sample contains an infinite number of points or as many as the number of points on a line segment, such as all possible heights, weights, etc., it is called a continuous random variable. Usually, continuous random variables represent measured data.

If a sample contains a finite number of points or an unending sequence with as many elements as there are whole numbers, then it is called a discrete random variable. Usually, discrete random variables represent count data.

Continuous data are usually measured. Discrete data are usually counted.

PARAMETERS AND STATISTICS

Numerical values describing a population are called parameters and numerical values describing a sample are called statistics.

	Parameter refers to population	Statistic refers to sample
Mean	μ	$\overline{X}$ (any letter with bar)
Variance	σ^2	s^2
Standard Deviation	σ	s (SD)

$$\text{Sum} = \Sigma$$

The mean ($\overline{X}$) of a set of scores equals the sum of the scores (ΣX) divided by the total number of scores (N). Each individual score or observation is denoted "X." The formula for the mean is:

$$\overline{X} = \frac{\Sigma X}{N}$$

The median is the middle score in a set; that is, the point above and below which 50% of the cases fall.

The mode is the most frequent score in a set.

1. Given the following sample 1, 2, 2, 2, 3, 3, 4, 4, 4, 5, 5, 6, 6, 6, 7 where ΣX = 60 (Sum of scores) N = 15 (Number of scores) Find: Median, mean.	
2. The range is the difference between the largest and smallest number in the set. Find the range of the following scores: 4, 4, 9, 2, 4, 11, 13, 8	Median = 4 Mean $= \dfrac{60}{15} = 4$
3. Find the mode of the preceding set of scores.	Range = 11

4. Given the following sample from a population
2, 2, 4, 4, 4, 5
where ΣX = 21 and N = 6
    Find:
        Median
        Mode
        Range
        Mean
	Mode = 4

	Median = 4 Mode = 4 Range = 3 Mean = 3.5

STANDARD DEVIATION

The standard deviation is an average of deviation scores or the root mean square deviation which describes the variability of the measures.

The summary of procedures for formula A is as follows:

(1) Calculate the mean.

(2) Subtract the mean from each raw score and square each result.

(3) Sum the squares.
(4) Divide the sum of squares by N − 1.
(5) Take the square root.

Form A

$$s = \sqrt{\frac{\Sigma(X - \overline{X})^2}{N - 1}}$$

Form B

$$s = \sqrt{\frac{(N \Sigma X^2) - (\Sigma X)^2}{N(N - 1)}}$$

Form C

$$s = \sqrt{\frac{\Sigma X^2 - \dfrac{(\Sigma X)^2}{N}}{N - 1}}$$

The standard deviation formulas given above yield approximately the same numerical value; however, the B and C forms are computational derivatives of the A form. These formulas (especially B and C) will be used in the computation of *t* tests later in the next program.

The standard deviation (s) is the square root of the variance (s^2).

Another way of expressing this fact is $s = \sqrt{s^2}$

The variance (s^2) is the standard deviation squared. $(s)^2$

If s equals **Form A** of the standard deviation formulas, then the variance (s^2) equals:

$$s^2 = \frac{\Sigma(X - \overline{X})^2}{N - 1}$$

5. If s = 5, then s^2 = _____ .	
6. If s^2 = 9, then s = _____ .	25
7. Using **Form A** of the standard deviation formulas, find the standard deviation and the variance of the following scores: 4, 4, 5, 5, 5, 6, 6, 7, 8, 10 where ΣX = 60, N = 10	3
8. Using **Form B** of the standard deviation formulas, find the standard deviation and the variance of the following scores: 4, 4, 5, 5, 5, 6, 6, 7, 8, 10 where ΣX = 60, N = 10	$\overline{X}$ = 6 $\Sigma (X - \overline{X})^2$ = 32 s = 1.89 s^2 = 3.56
9. The variance of a set of observations is unchanged if a constant is added to or subtracted from every score.	s = 1.89 s^2 = 3.56
10. If every observation is either multiplied or divided by a constant, then the variance is multiplied or divided by the square of the constant.	
11. If the variances of two random variables are added together or subtracted, then the resulting variance is equal to the sum of the two variances.	

t of reading scores is 10. If a constant of 5 is ︙re, what is the variance of the resulting set of ︙, 100, none	
︙ce of a set of reading scores is 10. If each score is ︙d by 2, then what is the variance of the resulting set of ︙20, 30, 40, 50, none	10
︙he variance of a set of MAT scores is 16. If each score has 2 subtracted from it, what is the resulting variance?	40
︙. Suppose that the variances of two random variables L and M are 2 and 3 respectively. What is the variance of the new distribution L and M? 2, 3, 5, 6, 12, 13, 36	16
16. Given the following sample, find s^2. 2, 3, 5, 7, 8	5
17. Add 3 to each of the scores in the preceding problem and find the new s^2.	$\Sigma X = 25$ $\overline{X} = 5,\ N = 5$ $\Sigma(X - \overline{X})^2 = 26$ $s^2\quad = 6.5$
18. Multiply each of the above scores by 2 and find the resulting variance.	$s^2\quad = 6.5$
	$s^2\quad = 26$

STANDARD SCORES AND Z SCORES

A Z score is a type of standard score. There are many different standard scores (G.R.E., C.E.E.B., Stanford-Binet, etc.).* Any standard score is a linear transformation representing the distance and direction a score is from the mean of a normal distribution.

If the mean of a distribution is 33, the score of 43 represents 10 points above the mean; but, 43 does not give a clear estimation of where that score lies in relation to the rest of the scores within a distribution. The standard deviation is a unit of measurement within a distribution. Knowing that a score of 43 is one standard deviation from the mean indicates a position in relation to the entire population.

A Z score equal to 1 represents a distance of one standard deviation from the mean. A Z score is defined by the following formula:

$$Z = \frac{X - \overline{X}}{s}$$

A Z score is the difference between the score you are observing and the mean, divided by the standard deviation.

Thus, the Z score represents a linear transformation of a score within one distribution to another distribution which has a mean equal to zero and a standard deviation equal to one.

*(See next page for a chart of a normal curve with approximations among several derived scores. This chart is also found in the parent text, page 102.)

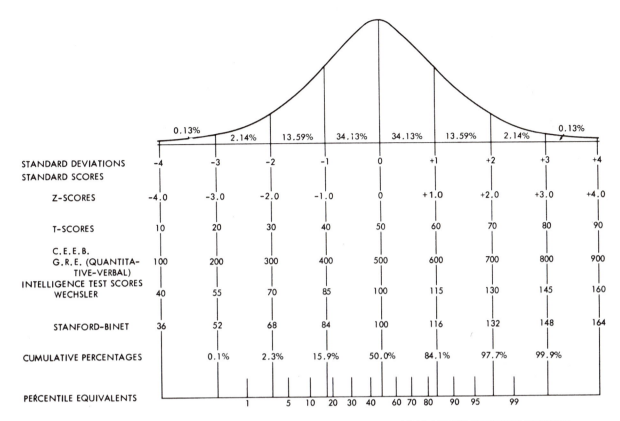

	0.13%	2.14%	13.59%	34.13%	34.13%	13.59%	2.14%	0.13%
STANDARD DEVIATIONS STANDARD SCORES	−4	−3	−2	−1	0	+1	+2	+3	+4
Z-SCORES	−4.0	−3.0	−2.0	−1.0	0	+1.0	+2.0	+3.0	+4.0
T-SCORES	10	20	30	40	50	60	70	80	90
C.E.E.B. G.R.E. (QUANTITA-TIVE-VERBAL)	100	200	300	400	500	600	700	800	900
INTELLIGENCE TEST SCORES WECHSLER	40	55	70	85	100	115	130	145	160
STANFORD-BINET	36	52	68	84	100	116	132	148	164
CUMULATIVE PERCENTAGES		0.1%	2.3%	15.9%	50.0%	84.1%	97.7%	99.9%	
PERCENTILE EQUIVALENTS		1	5 10 20 30 40	60 70 80 90 95	99			

NORMAL CURVE WITH APPROXIMATIONS AMONG DERIVED SCORES*

A table of *Z* scores represents areas under the normal curve which are associated with values equal to observed values of *Z*.

A *Z* score table is in the Appendix under Table A, page 123.

The percentage of cases under the normal distribution by standard deviations is given in the following table. Note that 34.13% of the area under the curve lies between the mean and the first standard deviation.

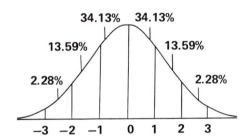

PROPERTIES OF THE NORMAL CURVE

Observations tend to cluster at the mean. Thus, the mode, which is the point on the horizontal axis where the curve is a maximum, occurs at the mean.

*From *Experimental Research in Music* by Madsen and Madsen, p. 102. (1970) Prentice-Hall, Inc. Used by permission of the authors and publishers.

The curve is symmetric about a vertical axis through the mean. For example, the height of the curve at $X = \overline{X} + 2s$ is exactly the same as the height of the curve at $X = \overline{X} - 2s$. As a result of this symmetry it can be seen that the mean, median, and mode are identical in a normal population.

The normal curve approaches the horizontal axis asymptotically. That is, the curve continues to decrease in height as it proceeds in either direction away from the mean but never quite reaches the horizontal axis. In practice, the area beyond $\overline{X} \pm 3s$ is negligible.

The total area under the curve and above the horizontal axis is equal to 1 or 100%.

19. In a table of standard scores the mean of the distribution equals zero and the standard deviations correspond to the Z numbers. (See Z table in Appendix, Table A.)	
20. Therefore, one can say that one-half of the scores in a distribution fall below the mean and one-half above.	
21. The mean of a distribution is equal to a Z score of _____ .	
22. Looking at a table of "Areas Under the Normal Curve" it is seen that the area under the curve corresponding to Z = 0.00 is _____ .	0
23. Since a Z value of 0.00 is only half (.5000) of the curve the total area under the normal curve is .0000, .5000, .9999, 1.0000	.5000
24. Therefore, it can be said about an obtained Z (0.00) that if _____ of the scores fall below "Z" and _____ fall above; that Z score is the_____ .	1.000
25. Looking at the Z table (Appendix, Table A), it can be seen that the areas under the normal curve given in that table represent the portion of the curve occurring to the right of the mean, i.e., in a one-tailed, positive direction. Since the Z table in the Appendix represents only one-half of the normal curve, it is labelled a _____ - _____ table.	1/2 1/2 mean
26. A minus Z score indicates standard deviations to the left of the mean, and a plus Z value indicates standard deviations to the right of the mean.	One-tailed
27. The area in the extreme positive tail corresponds to letter _____ in the diagram below; while the extreme negative end is represented by the letter _____ .	

28. The Z table (in Appendix) gives the Z score and the corresponding area or percentage under the normal curve which falls beyond that Z score. For example, if the Z score is +.5, then .3085 or 30.85% of the curve falls to the *right* of Z score .5. If a Z score is −1, then .1587 or 15.87% of the normal curve exists to the *left* of Z score −1. (Note diagram below.)

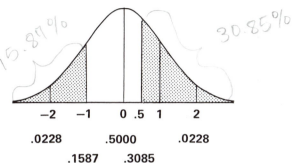

E, A

−2 −1 0 .5 1 2	
.0228 .5000 .0228	
.1587 .3085	

29. If a Z score of -2.00 is equal to .0228 of the area of the normal curve to the *left* of that score, what is the area to the *right* of a Z score +2.00? _____

30. If one wanted to know the area of the normal curve to the *right* of +1.00 Z score, the Z table value is .1584 or 15.84%. But if one wanted to know the area of the normal curve to the *left* of +1.00 Z score, then one would subtract .1584 from 1.0000.

    1.0000 total area under normal curve
−   .1584 area to the right of +1.00 Z score
    .8416 area to the left of +1.00 Z score

.0228

31. If one wanted to know the area of the normal curve to the right of +1.96, the Z table gives what value? (see Appendix) ._____

32. To obtain the area of the normal curve to the left of Z score +1.96, subtract the table value from 1.0000. The answer is ._____

.0250

33. What percentage of the area under the normal curve is between a Z score of −1.96 and +1.96? The area sought is

A, B, C, AB, AC, BC, ABC

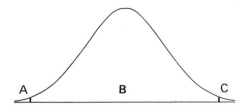

.9750

34. What percentage of the area under the normal curve lies outside of the area between the Z scores —2.575 and +2.575? The area sought is A, B, C, AB, AC, BC 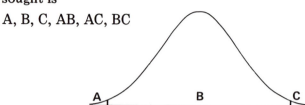	95% B
35. *t* values represent standard deviations just as Z values do. The areas under the normal curve for all possible t values would require many pages of values; therefore, the area under the curve is given at the top of the columns and the t values themselves are given in the body of the table.	1% AC
36. It should be noted that the t values are dependent upon degrees of freedom (usually df = N — 1). When the df (degrees of freedom) equal infinity, the t values are identical to Z values.	
37. For instance, a t = 1.96, df = infinity, corresponds to .0250 of the normal curve as does a Z value of _____	
38. In a one-tailed test only the area at one end of the curve is involved. A typical one-tailed test at the .05 level would have the following characteristics: 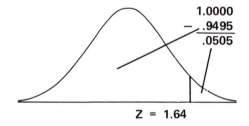	1.96
39. A two-tailed test would divide the area (α = 5%) between the two tails and would look like the example below: 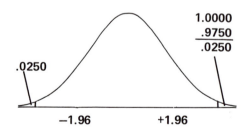	
40. From the example above, if one tail has .0250 or 2.5% of the area under the normal curve, then the area of two tails would equal _____ .	

41. The standard deviation of a group of scores is 5. The mean is 35. The Z score of a student who received a score of 25 is _____.	.0500 or 5%
42. The standard deviation of a group of scores is 7. The mean is 42. The Z score of a student who received a score of 56 is _____.	−2.00
43. The standard deviation of a group of scores is 4. The mean is 20. What is the area under the normal curve to the left of a score of 10?	+2.00
44. What percentage of the students in the preceding problem received a score higher than 10?	.0062

REVIEW *Sora — Aru* *SD*

45. Given the following sample data 11, 10, 9, 8, 7, 6, 5, 4, 3 find the Z scores of the following observed scores 10 3	99.38% 2.74
46. Suppose you had a sample of size 200 from a normally distributed population. How many cases would be expected to exceed each of the following Z scores? .20 1.80 −2.04 .53	1.095 −1.46
47. Given a normal population with $\overline{X} = 50$ and $s = 10$, find the probability of getting a score between 45 and 62.	84 7 196 60
48. A certain type of pad on a student-model clarinet lasts on the average 3.0 years, with a standard deviation of 0.5 year. Assuming the life of all such clarinet pads fits a normal distribution, find the probability that a given pad will last less than 2.3 years.	57.64%
49. An electrical firm manufactures light bulbs for metronomes that have a length of life that is normally distributed with a mean equal to 800 hours and a standard deviation of 40 hours. Find the probability that a bulb will burn between 778 and 834 hours.	.0808 2.3 3 s = 0.5 $Z = \dfrac{X - \overline{X}}{s}$

s = 40

778 834
800

50. On a music history examination the average grade was 74 and the standard deviation was 7. If 12% of the class are given a grade of A, and the grades are curved to follow a normal distribution, what is the lowest possible A and the highest possible B?

.8023
−.2912
.5111

Note: The preceding examples were solved by going first from a value of X to a Z score and then computing the desired area. In this problem we reverse the process and begin with a known area or probability, find the Z value, and then determine X from the formula $X = sZ + \overline{X}$.

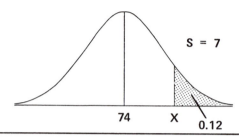

Lowest A = 82
Highest B = 81

CONFIDENCE INTERVALS

Suppose a random sample is taken from some population and the mean of that sample is 70. However, it can be hypothesized that the "real" population mean is 74. How can a probability statement be made about where the "real" mean actually lies? In the past, whenever a probability statement was made about some score, some form of the Z score was used. Probably, however, in individual scores the Z score formula was $Z = \dfrac{X - \overline{X}}{s}$ where X was the person's score, $\overline{X}$ was the sample mean and s was the sample standard deviation.

Now, since a sample mean (a statistic, $\overline{X}$) and a hypothesized population mean (a parameter, mu) are being used, the standard deviation of the sampling distribution (the standard error of the mean) must be calculated. Therefore, the appropriate Z score formula becomes $Z = \dfrac{\overline{X} - mu}{S_{\overline{X}}}$ where $\overline{X}$ is the sample mean, mu is the hypothesized population mean and $S_{\overline{X}}$ is the standard error of the mean, or standard deviation of the sampling distribution.

$S_{\overline{X}}$ is computed by the following formula $S_{\overline{X}} = \dfrac{s}{\sqrt{N}}$ where s is the sample standard deviation and N is the number of people in the sample. The intervals can now be calculated within which the "real" population mean would be expected to fall either 95 times out of 100 or 99 times out of 100. The limits for these intervals are called the 5% and 1% confidence limits. Levels of significant *differences* which occur outside these confidence intervals are also referred to as .05 and .01 levels of significance.

The 5% confidence limits for the problem with a mean of 40 in the sample of 144 people with a standard deviation of s = 15.6 can be calculated. To compute $S_{\overline{X}} = \dfrac{S}{\sqrt{N}} = \dfrac{15.6}{\sqrt{144}} = 1.3$

The normal probability table (Z table in Appendix) indicates that the Z score which cuts off 2.5% of the area in each tail of the normal curve is 1.96.

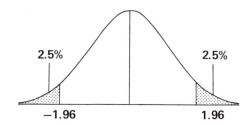

Altogether, then, a Z of 1.96 taken on both sides of the mean represents 95% of the area under the normal curve. Thus, a Z score of 1.96 can be translated into a mean score value. The intervals on both sides of the mean will indicate the area within which the "real" mean of the population falls 95% of the time. This is done by the following formula:

$$5\% \text{ confidence interval} = \overline{X} \pm (1.96) (S_{\overline{X}})$$

That is, taking the standard error of the mean ($S_{\overline{X}}$) and multiplying it by 1.96 a mean value will be obtained. Taking that distance above and below the sample mean, an interval will result within which the "real" population mean will fall 95% of the time.

$$
\begin{aligned}
5\% \text{ confidence interval} &= \overline{X} \pm (1.96) (S_{\overline{X}}) \\
&= 70 \pm (1.96) (1.3) \\
&= 70 \pm 2.55
\end{aligned}
$$

The 5% confidence interval is 67.45 through 72.55.

The statement can be made that 95 times out of a hundred, taking a sample of 144 people from some population, the sample mean will be within 2.55 points of the "real" population mean.

The same procedure applies for the 1% confidence limits. This time, the Z score that corresponds to an area of 99% of the normal curve taken on both sides of the mean is Z = 2.58.

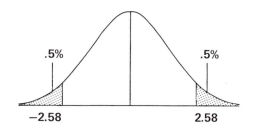

$$
\begin{aligned}
1\% \text{ confidence limits} &= \overline{X} \pm (2.58) (S_{\overline{X}}) \\
&= 70 \pm (2.58) (1.3) \\
&= 70 \pm 3.35 \\
&= 66.65 \text{ through } 73.35
\end{aligned}
$$

Naturally the confidence interval for the 1% level is larger than that of the 5% confidence interval because 99% of the area under the normal curve is included.

The statement can be made that 99 times out of a hundred, taking a sample of 144 people from some population, the sample mean value will be within 3.35 points of the "real" population mean value. One time out of a hundred it will be further away from the "real" population mean.

The basic method behind inferential statistics is much the same as the situations just discussed. Often one can hypothesize some value of a population parameter, or sample statistic, take an actual sample, compute some kind of Z score and make a probability statement on the chances of getting a result like that of the sample if the hypothesis were true. From this probability statement it can be inferred that certain things are true about the population or sample. One doesn't get *the* correct answer: one gets some information on which to base a decision.

51. One brand of valve oil used by brass players is manufactured so that the amount of oil in all containers is approximately normally distributed with a standard deviation equal to 0.5 ounce. Find the 95% confidence interval for the mean of all containers produced if a random sample of 36 containers had an average content of 7.4 ounces of valve oil.	
52. A random sample of 8 oboe reeds of a certain brand has an average weight of 18.6 grams and a standard deviation of 2.4 grams. Construct a 99% confidence interval for the true average weight of this particular brand of oboe reeds.	$7.24 < \overline{X} < 7.56$
53. The heights of a random sample of 50 college band students showed a mean of 68.5 inches and a standard deviation of 2.7 inches. Construct a 98% confidence interval for the mean height of all college students.	$16.4 < \overline{X} < 20.79$
54. Given a sample with the following data: $\overline{X} = 70 \quad s = 15 \quad N = 100$ Set up the following 1% confidence limits 5% confidence limits Make appropriate probability statements interpreting the confidence limits	$67.61 < \overline{X} < 69.39$
55. The Following Three Pages are Review Frames. Study Them and Take the Posttest. **Diagram for Frames 56-60** 	$66.13 - 73.87$ $67.06 - 72.94$ 99 (95) times out of 100, if I take a sample of size N from some population, the sample mean value will be within 3.87 (2.94) points of the true population mean value. One (5) time out of 100 it will be further away.
56. Which point represents $\overline{X}$?	
57. Which point represents the standard deviation?	C
58. Which point represents +2s?	G
59. Which point represents a Z score of about 1.5?	F
60. Which point represents a Z score of −2.0?	E

61. Given: a group of 64 Stanford Achievement test scores that are normally distributed with the group average being 50 and a standard deviation of 10. **Diagram for Frames 61-66** 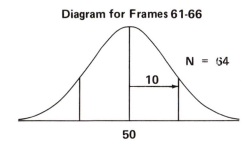 Find the Z score corresponding to a raw score of 25.	A
62. Find the probability of obtaining a score between 60 and 40.	—2.5
63. Find the raw score such that 33% of the scores fall below that point.	.6826
64. Find the raw score such that 9% of the scores fall above that point.	45.6
65. Calculate the number of observations that fall below a raw score of 40.	63.4
66. Calculate the number of observations that fall between the scores of 40 and 60.	10
67. The probability of not making a Type II error is called 1. significance level 2. confidence limit 3. power 4. bias 5. standard error	43.69
68. The probability of making a Type I error is completely controlled by the 1. confidence interval 2. power 3. bias 4. significance level 5. randomness	3
69. Rejecting an hypothesis as being false, when in fact it is true, is an example of 1. Type I error 2. Type II error 3. Type III error 4. Standard error 5. Sampling bias	4

70. Accepting an hypothesis as being true, when in fact it is false, is an example of making a
   1.   Type I error
   2.   Type II error
   3.   Type III error
   4.   Standard error
   5.   Sampling bias
	1

71. Accepting an hypothesis as being true, when in fact it is true, is an example of
   1.   Type I error
   2.   Type II error
   3.   Type III error
   4.   Standard error
   5.   None
	2

72. If a sample is not representative of the population from which it comes it is said to be a
   1.   random sample
   2.   biased sample
   3.   stratified sample
   4.   skewed sample
   5.   correlated sample
	5

73. If a sample is made up of 37 people, each subset of N = 37 which had an equal and independent chance of being chosen from the population, the sample is said to be
   1.   a random sample
   2.   a biased sample
   3.   a stratified sample
   4.   a skewed sample
   5.   a correlated sample
	2

74. Given a sample of 100 scores with a mean of 50 and a standard deviation of 15 compute the standard error of the mean	1
75. and the 5% confidence limits, and	1.5
76. write an appropriate probability statement interpreting the 5% confidence limits found in the preceding question.	47.06 - 52.94
77. You Have Now Completed a Program in Basic Statistics. Now Take the Posttest.	95 times out of 100, if one takes a sample of 100 from a population, the sample mean value will be within 2.94 points of the "real" population mean value. 5 times out of 100 it will be further away

V

A Programmed Guide to Common Statistical Tests

INSTRUCTIONS

1. Carefully read each explanation.*
2. Work musical example.
3. Use blank **Form** for future research analysis.

Explanations and formulas for the following program are taken in part from Nonparametric Statistics for the Behavioral Sciences by Sidney Siegel, 1956, McGraw-Hill Book Company. Appreciation to Mr. Siegel's fine text is herein acknowledged.

Musical examples are added to this program to ease the direct application of statistical analyses to experimentation in music.

CONTENTS

χ^2 (Chi-Square) One-Sample Test

Tests: "Goodness-of-Fit" technique which compares observed data (such as, objects, responses, or observations) to expected data. . . .*Goodness-of-fit* asks, "How well does the obtained value fit the expected value?"

Level of Measurement: Nominal

Hypotheses: H_0: Observed = expected
H_1: Observed $\neq$ expected

Formula: $\chi^2 = \Sigma \dfrac{(O - E)^2}{E}$ O = observed frequency
E = expected frequency

---

*A Supplementary Appendix includes a Glossary of Statistical Symbols, a Review of Basic Mathematics, and a Guide to Reading Statistical Tables. A quick overview of the Appendix is recommended before starting this program. Using a calculator will simplify completion of this program (see Use of a Burroughs Calculator, p. 120).

Procedure:

1. Put observed frequencies in category cells (A,B,C, ...) in the χ^2 Observed/Expected Table.
2. To obtain the expected frequencies, add all the observed cells and divide by the number of categories.

   $E = \dfrac{\Sigma \, O\text{'s}}{N}$ (Note: If the expected score is less than 5, do *not* use this statistical test.)

3. Complete χ^2 formula by computing each category and adding all values to obtain χ^2.
4. Degrees of freedom = number of categories minus one; df = $k - 1$.
5. Check χ^2 Table in Appendix. If the obtained χ^2 value has a probability equal to or less than α, reject H_0.

Example: Three brands of orange juice: A, B, C. 60 people pick the brand they like best. H_0 = no difference in o.j. preference. H_1 = there is a preference. df = $3 - 1 = 2$.

χ^2 **OBSERVED/EXPECTED TABLE**

Frequencies   **A**   **B**   **C** = Categories

	A	B	C
Observed = 0 =	24	19	17
Expected = E =	20	20	20

$$\chi^2 = \Sigma \, \frac{(0-E)^2}{E}$$

$$= \frac{(24-20)^2}{20} + \frac{(19-20)^2}{20} + \frac{(17-20)^2}{20}$$

$$= \frac{16}{20} + \frac{1}{20} + \frac{9}{20} = \frac{26}{20}$$

$$\chi^2 = 1.3$$

When df = 2 and α = .05, Chi Square Table gives the critical value as 5.99. The obtained value of 1.3 has a .50 probability of occurring. Since .50 probability is greater than .05 probability, fail to reject H_0.

Musical Example

χ^2 **(Chi-Square) One-Sample Test**

Nominal Data

Research Design: Forty music majors were asked to name their "favorite" composer of all times from a list of four composers: Bach, Beethoven, Brahms or Mozart.

Hypotheses: H_0: Observed = expected
              H_1: Observed $\neq$ expected

Significance Level: α = <u>.05</u> k = <u>4</u> (categories)   df = (k $-$ 1) = *3*

Procedure:

1. Fill in frequencies and compute formula.

χ^2 **OBSERVED/EXPECTED TABLE**

Frequencies   **A**   **B**   **C**   **D** = Categories

	A	B	C	D
Observed = 0 =	13	8	12	7
Expected = E =	10	10	10	10

χ^2 **FORMULA**

$$\chi^2 = \Sigma \frac{(0-E)^2}{E}$$

2. Compare obtained value to critical value in Chi-Squared Table (Appendix)

   Obtained χ^2 = _____

   Tabled α value = _____

3. If Tabled value equal to or less than the set α value (.05) then reject H_o, otherwise fail to reject H_o.

Statistical Decision:

Experimental Decision:

_____

χ^2 = 2.6   p > .30 fail to reject H_o

F O R M
χ^2 **(Chi-Square) One-Sample Test**
Nominal Data

Research Design:

Hypotheses: H_o:

          H_1:

Significance Level: α = . _____ k = _____ (categories)

          df = k − 1 = _____

Procedure

1. Fill in frequencies and compute formula.

χ^2 **OBSERVED/EXPECTED TABLE**

Frequencies

| | A | B | C | D | E | F | = Categories |

Observed = 0 =

Expected = E =

$$E = \frac{\Sigma\, O}{k}$$

χ^2 **FORMULA**

$$\chi^2 = \Sigma\, \frac{(O-E)^2}{E}$$

2. Compare obtained value to critical value in Chi-Squared Table.

   Obtained value = _____

   Tabled α value = _____

3. If Tabled value equal to or less than set α level of significance, reject H_o, otherwise fail to reject.

Statistical Decision:

Experimental Decision:

χ^2 **Two-Sample, Dependent Test**

Tests: McNemar Test for significance of changes is used when two categories are related . . . however, may not be related in same kind of measurement . . . good when subject acts as own control . . . usually a before-and-after temporal design.

Level of Measurement: Nominal

Hypotheses: H_o: There is no difference between two groups' represented population distributions.

H_1: There is a difference between two groups' represented population distributions.

Table: Fourfold Table for χ^2 Two Dependent Sample Test.

A score of an individual is placed in cell A if it changed from + to −, in cell B if it remained positive, in cell D if changed from − to +, or in cell C if remained negative.

df = 1 (degrees of freedom in χ^2 2 x 2 or fourfold tests always = 1)

(In this formula |A − D| means the absolute value of A − D, *regardless of sign:* |20 − 35| = 15.)

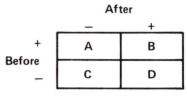

Formula: $\chi^2 = \dfrac{(|A-D|-1)^2}{A+D}$

Procedure:

1. Put observed frequencies in fourfold table.
2. Determine expected frequencies in cells A and D with this expectancy formula:

$$E = 1/2(A + D)$$

   If expected frequency <5, do not use this test, (use binomial).

3. Compute χ^2 value using formula.
4. Determine probability under H_0 for the obtained χ^2 value on the χ^2 critical Table. (Halve tabled probability for one-tailed test.) If *p* with df = 1 is equal to or less than α, reject H_0.

χ^2 **Two-Sample, Dependent Test**
Example

Experiment: 80 music majors were asked whether or not they favored listening to rock music at 110 dB. level of loudness. Next they were shown a short film on physical effects of loud sound on the human ear. After the film, the students were asked the initial question again.

Table
Music Majors' Position on Listening to Rock

After

	−	+
+	A 40	B 25
−	C 10	D 5

Before   df = 1

Expected Frequencies: In cells A and D: (greater than 5).

$$E = 1/2(A + D) = 1/2(40 + 5) = 22.5$$

Formula:

$$\chi^2 = \frac{(|A-D|-1)^2}{A+D}$$

$$= \frac{(40-5-1)^2}{40+5} = \frac{(35-1)^2}{45}$$

$$\chi^2 = 25.69$$

Chi-Square Table: The probability = .001 of this happening by chance alone. (one out of a thousand it could occur just by chance).

Statistical Decision: Would reject H_o that both groups come from the same population distribution. Favor H_1 that groups come from different population distributions.

Experimental Decision: Since there is a statistically significant difference in both groups of responses (before and after), the film variable seems to make a difference on how those music majors viewed listening to rock music.

Musical Example
F O R M
χ^2 Two Sample Dependent Test

Research Design: A pre-posttest questionnaire asked 40 music history students if they preferred music of the Renaissance to that of the Middle Ages. A 30 minute lecture was given between questioning and stressed the unique beauty of the Middle Ages' music compared to that of the Renaissance.

Hypotheses: H_o: There is no difference in the "before and after" represented populations.

$\quad\quad\quad\quad$ H_1: There is a difference in the "before and after" represented populations.

Significance Level: α = .05 df = 1, Nominal data.

Procedure:

1. Put observed frequencies in fourfold table:

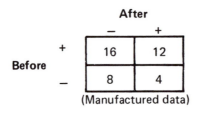

(Manufactured data)

2. Determine expected frequencies in cells A and D. (If the expected frequency <5, do not use χ^2 test, use binominal).

$\quad\quad$ E = 1/2(A + D) = _____

3. Compute χ^2 value using formula:

$$\chi^2 = \frac{(|A - D| - 1)^2}{A + D}$$

4. Determine the probability under H_o for the obtained χ^2 value on the χ^2 Table. (Halve tabled probability for one-tailed test).

$\quad\quad$ Obtained value $\quad$ = _____

$\quad\quad$ Tabled probability = _____

Statistical Decision: (If p with df = 1 is equal to or less than the designated α reject H$_o$.):

Experimental Decision:

$$\overline{\chi^2 = 6.05 \quad p > .02 \quad \text{Reject H}_o}$$

F O R M
χ^2 Two-Sample Dependent Test

Research Design:

Hypotheses: H$_o$:

        H$_1$:

Significance Level: α = _____ df = 1, Nominal data.

Procedure:

1. Put observed frequencies in fourfold table:

2. Determine expected frequencies in cells A and D. (If the expected frequency <5, do not use χ^2 test, use binominal).

     E = 1/2(A + D) = _____

3. Compute χ^2 value using formula:

$$\chi^2 = \frac{(|A - D| - 1)^2}{A + D}$$

4. Determine the probability under H$_o$ for the obtained χ^2 value on the χ^2 Table. (Halve tabled probability for one-tailed test).

     Obtained value   = _____

     Tabled probability   = _____

Statistical Decision: (If p with df = 1 is equal to or less than the designated α, reject H$_o$.):

Experimental Decision:

χ^2 Test for Two Independent Samples

Tests: Two Independent samples observed under two conditions (2 X 2 table) or k (more than two) conditions.

Level of Measurement: Nominal

Hypotheses: H_o: No difference between two groups or rows (as r_1 and r_2).

H_1: There is a difference between the two groups.

Tables:

χ^2 2 X 2 Contingency Table

A	B	A + B
C	D	C + D

A + C   B + D   N

df = 1

χ^2 $\underline{k}$ Conditions Table

	k_1	k_2	k_3	
r_1	O_1 E_1	O_2 E_2	O_3 E_3	Σr_1
r_2	O_1 E_1	O_2 E_2	O_3 E_3	Σr_2
	Σk_1	Σk_2	Σk_3	N

df = (r − 1) (k − 1)

Formulas:

$$\chi^2 = \frac{N\left(\left| AD - BC \right| - \frac{N}{2}\right)^2}{(A + B)\ (C + D)\ (A + C)\ (B + D)}$$

$$\chi^2 = \overset{r}{\Sigma}\ \overset{k}{\Sigma}\ \frac{(O - E)^2}{E}$$

Procedure:

1. Put observed frequencies in k X r contingency table....k = columns for groups, r = rows for conditions.

2. k Conditions Table *only*: determine expected frequency for each cell from the product of its marginal totals divided by N(total of *all* independent observations). For example E_1 for cell $r_1 k_1$ = $\frac{(\Sigma r_1)\ (\Sigma k_1)}{N}$ (upper left cell)

3. 2 X 2 Table: appropriate when N not less than 20.... When N is between 20 and 40, smallest frequency tolerable in each cell is 5.

4. Compute χ^2 by appropriate formula.

5. Check Chi-Square Table for significance of obtained χ^2 value. (For one-tailed test, divide significance level by 2). If tabled probability equal to or less than α, reject H_o.

χ^2 Two Independent Samples
Examples

1. **2 X 2 Contingency Table Model.**

   Problem: 2 Methods of teaching French, A and B. . . . Proficiency on test, pass or fail. . .

	A	B	
Pass	22	12	34
Fail	8	18	26
	30	30	60

   df = 1
   α = .05

$$\chi^2 = \frac{N\left(|AD - BC| - \frac{N}{2}\right)^2}{(A + B)(C + D)(A + C)(B + D)}$$

$$= \frac{60\left[|(22)(18) - (12)(8)| - \frac{60}{2}\right]^2}{(22 + 12)(8 + 18)(22 + 8)(12 + 18)}$$

$$= 5.50$$

Chi-Squared Table given p<.02 of obtaining χ^2 = 5.50 with df = 1 and α = .05. Decision: Reject H_o.

2. **k X r Contingency Table.**

   Problem: Smokers and nonsmokers; causes of death.

Death by:	Smokers		Non-Smokers		
Heart failure	30	26.6	20	23.3	50
Cancer	42	26.6	8	23.3	50
Other causes	8	26.6	42	23.3	50
	80		70		150

   df = (r − 1)(k − 1)
   = (3 − 1)(2 − 1)
   = 2

   α = .05

$$\chi^2 = \sum^r \sum^k \frac{(O - E)^2}{E}$$

$$= \frac{(30 - 26.6)^2}{26.6} + \frac{(20 - 23.3)^2}{23.3} + \frac{(42 - 26.6)^2}{26.6} +$$

$$\frac{(8 - 23.3)^2}{23.3} + \frac{(8 - 26.6)^2}{26.6} + \frac{(42 - 23.3)^2}{23.3}$$

$$= 47.89 \qquad p < .001 \text{ Reject } H_o$$

Musical Example
χ^2 Test for Two Independent Samples

Research Design: Two groups (undergraduate and graduate) of music students listened to five orchestral excerpts. They were asked to write if the tempi taken were faster, the same, or slower than they would have chosen to conduct. Famous recordings were disguised as done by amateur conductors.

Hypothesis: H_0: No difference between the groups' represented population distributions.

$\qquad\quad$ H_1: There is a difference between groups.

Significance Level: α = .05 for *2* groups and *3 k* conditions.

Tables: 2 × 2 Table $\qquad\qquad\qquad\qquad\qquad$ *k* Conditions Table

A	B
C	D

df = 1

	k_1	k_2	k_3	k_4
r_1	8	12	5	
r_2	3	4	8	
r_3				
r_4				
	11	16	13	

df = (r − 1) (k − 1) = _____

Formulas: $\qquad \chi^2 = \dfrac{N\left(\mid AD - BC \mid - \frac{N}{2}\right)^2}{(A + B)\,(C + D)\,(A + C)\,(B + D)}$ $\qquad\qquad \chi^2 = \overset{r}{\underset{\Sigma}{}}\,\overset{k}{\underset{\Sigma}{}}\,\dfrac{(O - E)^2}{E}$

Procedure:

1. Put observed frequencies in k × r contingency table.
2. If 2 × 2 table *not* used, determine expected frequency for each cell from the product of its marginal totals divided by N(total of *all* independent observations).
3. 2 × 2 table used when N not less than 20. . . . When N is between 20 and 40, smallest frequency tolerable in each cell is 5.
4. Compute χ^2 by appropriate formula.
5. Check Chi-Square Table for significance of obtained χ^2 value. Obtained value_____

$\qquad$ tabled p = . _____(for one-tailed test, divide significance level by 2). If tabled probability equal to or less than α, reject H_0.

Statistical Decision:

Experimental Decision:

$\overline{\qquad\chi^2 = 4.76 \ \ p > .05 \ \text{fail to reject}\qquad}$

χ^2 **Test for Two Independent Samples**

Research Design:

Hypotheses: H_0:

$\quad\quad\quad\quad\quad$ H_1:

Significance Level: α = . _____ for _____ groups and _____ *k* conditions.

Tables: 2 X 2 Table

k Conditions Table

	k_1	k_2	k_3	k_4
r_1				
r_2				
r_3				
r_4				

A	B
C	D

df = 1

$$df = (r - 1)(k - 1) = \underline{\quad\quad\quad}$$

Formulas:
$$\chi^2 = \frac{N\left(\mid AD - BC \mid - \frac{N}{2}\right)^2}{(A+B)\ (C+D)\ (A+C)\ (B+D)} \quad\quad \chi^2 = \overset{r}{\underset{\Sigma}{}} \overset{k}{\underset{\Sigma}{}} \frac{(O - E)^2}{E}$$

Procedure:
1. Put observed frequencies in k X r contingency table.
2. If 2 X 2 table *not* used, determine expected frequency for each cell from the product of its marginal totals divided by N(total of *all* independent observations).
3. 2 X 2 table used when N not less than 20. . . . When N is between 20 and 40, smallest frequency tolerable in each cell is 5.
4. Compute χ^2 by appropriate formula.
5. Check Chi-Square Table for significance of obtained χ^2 value. Obtained value_____

    tabled p = . _____ (for one-tailed test, divide significance level by 2). If tabled probability equal to or less than α, reject H_0.

Statistical Decision:

Experimental Decision:

Wilcoxon Matched-Pairs Signed-Ranks Test

Tests: Two matched pairs of small samples (under 25).

Level of Measurement: Ordinal or interval.

Function: Analyzes rank signs of difference scores . . . determines signed difference between two scores . . . nonparametric alternative to dependent t test . . . for small samples and ordinal data.

Hypotheses: H_0: There is no difference between number of plus and minus ranks.

H_1: A difference exists between number of + and − ranks, (two-tailed alternative). Or There are significantly more plus signs than minus signs, or vice versa, (one-tailed alternative).

Procedure:

1. For each matched pair, determine the signed difference (d) between the two scores. (for example: A − B = d, 42 − 71 = −29).
2. Rank d's without respect to sign. With tied d's, assign the average of the tied ranks.
3. Affix to each rank the sign (+ or −) of the d which it represents.
4. Determine T, the smaller number of like-signed ranks summed.

Example

Pair	A Score	B Score	d	Rank of d	Sum smaller rank
a	42	71	−29	−8	
b	60	75	−15	−6.5	
c	59	61	− 2	−1	
d	75	60	+ 15	6.5	6.5
e	66	59	+ 7	4	4
f	47	52	− 5	−2	
g	63	57	+ 6	3	3
h	55	63	− 8	−5	
					T = 13.5

5. The significance of the obtained T value depends on the size of N.
   a. If N ≤ 25, Table C (Appendix) shows critical T values for various sizes of N. . . . If observed T value is *equal to or less* than that given in the table for a particular significance level (.05 here) and size of N, H_0 is rejected at that level of significance.
   b. If N is larger than 25, compute the value of Z with a Z formula and determine its probability under H_0 in a normal distribution table. If the p obtained is equal to or less than α, reject H_0.

$$Z \text{ formula: } Z = \frac{T - \dfrac{N(N+1)}{4}}{\sqrt{\dfrac{N(N+1)(2N+1)}{24}}}$$

Example 5a

The obtained T = 13.5 with N = 8 is compared to the tabled T value of *4* (see Wilcoxon Table, in Appendix). Since the obtained T value is greater than critical T, the H_0 is not rejected.

Musical Example
Wilcoxon Matched-Pairs

Research Design: Ten applied students taped a jury-type performance. Group A, ten music students, judged the tapes by using a standard evaluation form. Group B, ten music faculty members, judged the tapes by using the same form.

Hypotheses: H_o: There is no difference between group evaluation distributions (i.e., between student-faculty evaluations).

H_1: There is a difference between group evaluation distributions or between student and faculty evaluations.

Statistical Test: Wilcoxon Matched-Pairs Signed-Ranks is utilized since there are two-matched pairs of small sample size (under 25).

Level of Significance: $\alpha = .05$ $N = 10$ (number of pairs).

Sampling Distribution: Samples with $N \leq 25$ have probabilities calculated in Wilcoxon Table.

When $N > 25$, probabilities are found on a normal curve Z Table.

Procedure:

1. List the matched-pairs' scores in the table below and determine the signed difference (d) between each two scores.

Students vs. Faculty Rating*   TABLE

Pair	A Score	B Score	d	Rank of d	Sum of smaller rank
1	98	100			
2	97	88			
3	70	85			
4	70	77			
5	62	68			
6	58	52			
7	44	35			
8	23	20			
9	17	15			
10	11	10			

*(Fabricated data)   T =

2. Rank d's without respect to sign. With tied d's assign the average of the tied ranks. Smallest d is number 1.
3. Affix to each rank the sign (+ or −) of the d which it represents.
4. Determine T, the *smaller* number of like-signed ranks summed.
5. Check appropriate Table for critical value.
    a.   If $N \leq 25$, Wilcoxon Table (Table C).
    b.   When $N > 25$, convert the obtained T to a Z score by computing the following Z formula . . . then check probability found in normal distribution Z Table (See Appendix, Table A).

Z Formula: Compute 5b. here:

$$Z = \frac{T - \dfrac{N\,(N + 1)}{4}}{\sqrt{\dfrac{N\,(N + 1)\,(2N + 1)}{24}}}$$

6. If obtained T value is equal to or less than value in Table C, H_o is rejected ... or ... if obtained *Z* value provides a tabled probability equal to or less than the alpha (α) selected, reject H_o.

When N =_____ , critical Table value for T = _____

or for Z = _____

7. Statistical Decision:

8. Experimental Decision:

T = 25   Fail to reject H_o

F O R M
Wilcoxon Matched-Pairs

Research Design:

Hypotheses: H_o:

H_1:

Statistical Test: Wilcoxon Matched-Pairs Signed-Ranks is utilized since there are two-matched pairs of small sample size (under 25).

Level of Significance: α = . _____N =_____ (number of pairs).

Sampling Distribution: Samples with N $\leq$ 25 have probabilities calculated in Wilcoxon Table.
When N > 25, probabilities are found on a normal curve *Z* Table.

Procedure:

1. List the matched-pairs' scores in the table below and determine the signed difference (d) between each two scores.

TABLE

Pair	A Score	B Score	d	Rank of d	Sum of smaller rank

T =

2. Rank d's without respect to sign. With tied d's assign the average of the tied ranks. Smallest d is number 1.

3. Affix to each rank the sign (+ or −) of the d which it represents.

4. Determine T, the *smaller* number of like-signed ranks summed.

5. Check appropriate Table for critical value.

   a. If $N \leq 25$, Wilcoxon Table (Appendix, Table C).

   b. When $N > 25$, convert the obtained T to a Z score by computing the following Z formula . . . then check probability found in normal distribution Z Table (See Appendix, Table A)

$$Z \text{ Formula: } Z = \frac{T - \frac{N(N+1)}{4}}{\sqrt{\frac{N(N+1)(2N+1)}{24}}}$$

6. If obtained T value is equal to or less than value in Table C, H_o is rejected ... or ... if obtained Z value provides a tabled probability equal to or less than the alpha (α) selected, reject H_o.

When N = _____ , critical Table value for T = _____

or for Z = _____

7. Statistical Decision:

8. Experimental Decision:

Mann-Whitney U Test

Tests: Two independent groups (usually smaller than 20 per group).

Level of Measurement: Ordinal

Function: Determines whether two independent groups have been drawn from the same population. ... Most powerful nonparametric test. ... Alternative to parametric *t* test. ... Avoids *t* test assumptions. ... Tests data weaker than interval level of measurement.

Hypotheses: H_o: Both groups are equal, i.e., both groups come from a common population distribution.

H_1: Groups are not equal; they do not come from a common population distribution.

Procedure:

1. Record the scores of both groups (n_1 and n_2).

   n_1 = number of smaller group.
   n_2 = number of larger group.

2. Rank all scores (taking both groups together) giving rank 1 to the lowest score. Assign tied observations the average of the tied ranks.

3. Sum the ranks for each group. R_1 = sum of ranks in group one, R_2 = sum of ranks in group two.

TABLE (example)
Scores and Ranks for Mann-Whitney U Test

Group I:	Scores	Rank	Group II:	Scores	Rank
	12	6.5		4	1
	15	9		7	2
	16	10		9	3
	17	11		10	4
	20	12.5		11	5
	23	15		12	6.5
		$R_1 = 64$		13	8
				20	12.5
				21	14
				27	16
					$R_2 = 72$

4. Use the data in the statistical U test. Find the smaller U value (compute both U values for R_1 and R_2).

$$U = n_1 n_2 + \frac{n_1 (n_1 + 1)}{2} - R_1 \qquad\bigg|\qquad U = n_1 n_2 + \frac{n_2 (n_2 + 1)}{2} - R_2$$

Examples:

$$U = (6)(10) + \frac{6(6+1)}{2} - 64 \qquad\bigg|\qquad U = (6)(10) + \frac{10(10+1)}{2} - 72$$

$$U = 60 + 21 - 64 \qquad\qquad\qquad\bigg|\qquad U = 60 + 55 - 72$$

$$U = 17 \qquad\qquad\qquad\qquad\quad\bigg|\qquad U = 43$$

Obtained value for U = 17.

5. Check the appropriate Mann-Whitney U Table for the critical value of U at the chosen α and size of n_1 and n_2.*

Example: assuming $\alpha = .05$ and $n_1 = 6$, $n_2 = 10$, a two-tailed critical value for $U = 11$.

6. Make statistical decision about H_0. If obtained value is equal to or less than the critical value, reject H_0.

Example: Since the obtained value of U = 17 is more than the critical value of $U = 11$, the decision is *not* to reject the H_0.

Conversion Formula (U to Z):

$$Z = \frac{U - \frac{n_1 n_2}{2}}{\sqrt{\frac{(n_1)(n_2)(n_1 + n_2 + 1)}{12}}}$$

Musical Example

FORM

Mann-Whitney U Test

Research Description: The effect of a metronome in playing an exercise (a selected musical excerpt) five times in a row without a mistake. 20 clarinetists served as subjects. The Experimental group (12) played a selected exercise to criterion with continual use of a metronome. A Control group (8) played the same exercise to criterion without reference to a metronome.

Hypotheses: H_0: The number of trials to criterion on playing a musical excerpt is the same for musicians playing with/without a metronome.

H_1: The number of trials to criterion in playing a musical excerpt is *not* the same for musicians playing with/without a metronome.

Statistical Test: Mann-Whitney U test is chosen because there are two independent groups, small samples, and ordinal data.

Significance Level: $\alpha = .05$ $n_1 = 8$ (smaller group).

$n_2 = 12$ (larger group)   (usually $n_2 \le 20$)

*(When sample size of $n_2 > 20$, convert U value to Z score and find critical Z value in the Normal Curve Table.)

Procedure:

1. Record the scores of both groups (n_1 and n_2).

   n_1 = number of smaller group. n_2 = number of larger group.

2. Rank all scores (taking both groups together) giving rank 1 to the lowest score. Assign tied observations the average of the tied ranks.

3. Sum the ranks for each group. R_1 = sum of ranks in group one, R_2 = sum of ranks in group two.

Scores and Ranks for Mann-Whitney U Test

Group I:	Scores	Rank	Group II:	Scores	Rank
	6			5	
	7			8	
	8			9	
	9			10	
	12			10	
	12			11	
	15			11	
	16			12	
				13	
				13	
				14	
				17	
	R_1 =			R_2 =	

4. Use the data in the statistical U test. Find the smaller U value by computing both U values for R_1 and R_2.

$$U = n_1 n_2 + \frac{n_1 (n_1 + 1)}{2} - R_1 \qquad U = n_1 n_2 + \frac{n_2 (n_2 + 1)}{2} - R_2$$

Obtained value for *smaller U* = _____

5. Check the appropriate Mann-Whitney U Table for the critical value of U at the chosen α and sample size.*

   When α = . _____ and n_1 = _____ and n_2 = _____ , the tabled critical value = _____ .

6. Make statistical decision about H_o. If obtained value is equal to or less than the critical value, reject H_o.

   Statistical Decision: _____

   Experimental Decision: _____

   _____ .

$$Z = \frac{U - \dfrac{n_1 n_2}{2}}{\sqrt{\dfrac{(n_1)(n_2)(n_1 + n_2 + 1)}{12}}}$$

$U = 43$ $p > .05$ Fail to reject H_o

*(When sample size of $n_2 > 20$, convert U value to Z score and find critical Z value in the Normal Curve Table).

FORM
Mann-Whitney U Test

Research Description:

Hypotheses: H_o:

$\qquad$ H_1:

Statistical Test: Mann-Whitney U test is chosen because there are two independent groups, small samples, and ordinal data.

Significance Level: α = . _____ $\qquad$ n_1 = _____ (smaller group).

$\qquad\qquad\qquad\qquad\qquad\qquad\qquad$ n_2 = _____ (larger group)

$\qquad\qquad\qquad\qquad\qquad\qquad\qquad\qquad$ (usually $n_2 \le 20$)

Procedure:

1. Record the scores of both groups (n_1 and n_2).

   n_1 = number of smaller group.

   n_2 = number of larger group.

2. Rank all scores (taking both groups together) give rank 1 to the lowest score. Assign tied observations the average of the tied ranks.

3. Sum the ranks for each group. R_1 = sum of ranks in group one, R_2 = sum of ranks in group two.

Scores and Ranks for Mann-Whitney U Test

Group I:	Scores	Rank	Group II:	Scores	Rank
R_1 =				R_2 =	

4. Use the data in the statistical U test. Find the smaller U value by computing both U values for R_1 and R_2.

$$U = n_1 n_2 + \frac{n_1 (n_1 + 1)}{2} - R_1 \qquad\qquad U = n_1 n_2 + \frac{n_2 (n_2 + 1)}{2} - R_2$$

Obtained value for *smaller* U = _____.

5. Check the appropriate Mann-Whitney U Table for the critical value of U at the chosen α and sample size.*

When α = ._____and n_1 =_____and n_2 = _____,

the tabled critical value =

6. Make statistical decision about H_o. If obtained value is equal to or less than the critical value, reject H_o.

Statistical Decision:_____

Experimental Decision:_____

_____

$$Z = \frac{U - \dfrac{n_1 n_2}{2}}{\sqrt{\dfrac{(n_1)(n_2)(n_1 + n_2 + 1)}{12}}}$$

Friedman Two-Way Analysis of Variance

Tests: k (more than two) matched samples . . . equal number of cases in each sample . . . matching may be achieved by (1) studying the same group of subjects under each of k conditions, or (2) with several sets with k matched subjects which are randomly assigned (one subject from each group to the first condition, another subject from each group to the second condition, etc.) . . . analysis on ranks, not raw scores.

Level of Measurement: At least ordinal.

Hypotheses: H_o: All samples come from the same population.

H_1: All samples do not come from the same population.

Procedure:

1. Place the scores in a two-way table having k columns (conditions) and N rows (subjects or groups).

Examples

Scores of Three Subjects Under Four Conditions

Subjects	Conditions			
	I	II	III	IV
Subject A	12	7	4	10
Subject B	9	8	5	11
Subject C	12	4	5	9

Matched-Sets of Subjects ** **Under Three Treatments**

Matched-Sets	Treatments		
	+	−	0
Set 1	X_1	X_2	X_3
Set 2	Y_1	Y_3	Y_2
Set 3	Z_3	Z_1	Z_2

**Randomly assigned in each block

*(When sample size of $n_2 > 20$, convert U value to Z score and find critical Z value in the Normal Curve Table.)

2. Rank the scores *across each row* from one to k. If k (the number of columns) = 4 (as in this case), scores would be ranked *across rows* from 1 to 4. For example, Group A scores *across the row* are 12, 7, 4, 10. Ranks across Group A row are 4, 2, 1, 3.

3. Sum the ranks in each column: R_j. examples 2 and 3:

Ranks of Three Subjects under Four Conditions

Subjects	Conditions			
	I	II	III	IV
Subject A	4	2	1	3
Subject B	3	2	1	4
Subject C	4	1	2	3
Rj	11	5	4	10

4. Compute the value of χ_r^2, the statistic in the Friedman Analysis.

Friedman Formula:

$$\chi_r^2 = \frac{12}{Nk\,(k\,+\,1)} \sum_{j\,=\,1}^{k} (Rj)^2 \,-\, 3\,N(k\,+\,1)$$

Formula Key: N = number of rows
k = number of columns
Rj = sum of ranks in each j column

$\sum_{j\,=\,1}^{k}$ = sum of squares of sums over all k conditions.

example 4:

$$\chi_r^2 = \frac{12}{(3)\,(4)\,(4\,+\,1)} \left[(11)^2 \,+\, (5)^2 \,+\, (4)^2 \,+\, (10)^2 \right] \,-\, (3)\,(3)\,(4\,+\,1)$$

$$= 7.4$$

5. To determine the probability of occurrence under H_o associated with the observed value of χ_r^2, consider the sizes of N and k:

   a. Friedman Table gives exact probabilities associated with values as large as an observed χ_r^2 for k = 3, N = 2 to 9, and for k = 4, N = 2 to 4.

   b. For N and/or k larger than those shown in the Friedman Table, the associated probability may be determined by reference to the Chi-Square Distribution Table with df = $k - 1$.

6. If the probability yielded by the appropriate method in step 5 is *equal to or less than alpha*, reject H_o.

> example 5 and 6: the obtained $\chi_r^2 = 7.4$.
>
> $k = 4$
> $N = 3$
>
> Using Table N, $p = .033$.
>
> Since alpha level of .05 is the criteria, .033 is less than .05 and the H_o is rejected.

Musical Example
Friedman Two-Way Analysis of Variance

Research Design: 30 college music students and music faculty were asked to rank their personal preference of composers from one to four (1 to 4). The composers were listed alphabetically: Bach, Barber, Mozart, and Stravinsky. Groups of ten were: A. Music undergraduates, B. Music graduates, and C. Music faculty.

Hypotheses: H_o: All groups will have the same distribution of scores or preferences (i.e., come from the same population).

> H_1: Groups will not have the same distribution of preference.

Statistical Test: The Friedman Two-Way Analysis of Variance was chosen because the data consist of small numbers of subjects and conditions measured at an ordinal level.

Significance Level: $\alpha = \underline{.05}$ $N = \underline{3}$ (number of groups or subjects).

> $k = \underline{4}$ (number of conditions).

Sampling Distribution: Probabilities for small N and k are found in the Friedman Table (Appendix). Probabilities for larger samples (when N is larger than 9) are located in the χ^2 (Chi-Square Table in the Appendix.

Procedure:

1. Place the scores in a two-way table having k columns (conditions) and N rows (subjects or groups).

GROUP SUMS FOR THREE GROUPS ACROSS FOUR CONDITIONS

Subjects*	Conditions			
	I	II	III	IV
A	24	29	24	23
B	12	37	20	33
C	14	37	16	33

*(Subjects here refer to group-generated data points).

2. Rank the scores across each *row* from one to *k*.
3. Sum the ranks in each column: R_j.

Ranks and Sums Table
Three Matched Groups under Four Conditions

Subjects	Conditions			
	I	II	III	IV
A	2.5	4	2.5	1
B	1	4	2	3
C	1	4	2	3
R_j =	+ _____	_____	_____	_____

4. Compute the value of χ_r^2 using the Friedman Formula:

$$\chi_r^2 = \frac{12}{N\ k\ (k+1)}\ \sum_{j=1}^{k} (Rj)^2 - 3\ N(k+1)$$

5. Check appropriate Table and probability value (Appendix). Friedman Table for small samples: χ^2 for larger.

Tabled p = _____

6. If the Tabled probability above is equal to or *less* than α, reject H_o.
7. Statistical Decision:

8. Experimental Decision:

$$\overline{\chi^2 = 6.10 \quad p > .075\ \text{fail to reject}\ H_o}$$

F O R M
Friedman Two-Way Analysis of Variance

Research Design:

Hypotheses: H_o:

   H_1:

Statistical Test: The Friedman Two-Way Analysis of Variance was chosen because the data consist of a small number of subjects and conditions measured at an ordinal level.

Level of Significance: α = . _____ N = _____ (number of groups or subjects).

   k = _____ (number of conditions).

Sampling Distribution: Probabilities for small N and k found in Friedman Table.

Probabilities for larger sample ($N > 9$) found in χ^2 Table.

Procedure:

1. Place the scores in a two-way table having k columns (conditions) and N rows (subjects or groups).

Subjects	Conditions			
	I	II	III	IV

2. Rank the scores across each *row* from one to k.
3. Sum the ranks in each column: R_j.

Ranks and Sums Table

Subjects	Conditions			
	I	II	III	IV
$R_j =$	____	____	____	____

4. Compute the value of χ_r^2 using the Friedman Formula:

$$\chi_r^2 = \frac{12}{N\,k\,(k+1)} \sum_{j=1}^{k} (Rj)^2 - 3\,N(k+1)$$

5. Check appropriate Table and probability value. Friedman Table for small samples; χ^2 for larger.

$$\text{Tabled p } = \underline{\hspace{4cm}}$$

6. If the Tabled probability above is equal to or less than α, reject H_o.

7. Statistical Decision:

8. Experimental Decision:

Kruskal-Wallis One-Way Analysis of Variance

Tests: Whether k independent samples represent the same population . . . one-way analysis of variance by ranks.

Level of Measurement: At least ordinal.

Function: Compares the sum of rank scores among k groups . . . alternative to independent t test or parametric one-way analysis of variance.

Hypotheses: H_o: There is no difference in scores among k groups.

H_1 : There is a difference in scores among k groups.

Procedure:

1. Rank all of the observations for k groups in a single series, assigning ranks from 1 to N.

2. Determine the value of R (sum of ranks) for each of k groups by ranks. Next find the mean of each rank, $\bar{R}$, by computing $R/n = \bar{R}$, for example: $\bar{R}_1 = 26/5 = 5.2$.

Example Table

Group 1		Group 2		Group 3	
Score	Rank	Score	Rank	Score	Rank
60	6	89	10	50	4
48	3	90	11	57	5
45	2	97	12	42	1
72	8	78	9		
66	7				
Sums: R_1 = 26		R_2 = 42		R_3 = 10	
$\bar{R}_1$ = 5.2		$\bar{R}_2$ = 10.5		$\bar{R}_3$ = 3.3	

Tied scores between two or more scores are assigned the mean of the ranks for which it is tied, for example:

N = 12

Score	Rank	Calculation (counting)
4	1	1
8	2	2
11	3.5	(3 + 4)/2
11	3.5	
12	5	5
15	7	(6 + 7 + 8)/3
15	7	
15	7	
20	9	9
25	10	10

3. Compute the value of H with the Kruskal-Wallis formula:

$$H = \frac{12}{N(N+1)} \; \Sigma \frac{R^2}{n} - 3(N+1) \qquad \Sigma = \text{sum of ranks squared over number in group}$$

Example taken from Table:

$$H = \frac{12}{12(12+1)} \left[\frac{(26)^2}{5} + \frac{(42)^2}{4} + \frac{(10)^2}{3} \right] - 3(12+1)$$

$$H = 9.76$$

If several scores are tied, compute the value of H with this formula:

$$H = \frac{\dfrac{12}{N(N+1)} \; \Sigma \dfrac{R^2}{n} - 3(N+1)}{1 - \dfrac{\Sigma T}{N^3 - N}}$$

where $T = t^3 - t$ (when t is the number of tied observations in a tied group of scores)

N = number of observations in all k samples together (sum of all n's).

ΣT = sum ties over all groups.

4. To find significance of the obtained H value use the appropriate Table:
   a. If $k = 3$ and if n_1, n_2, $n_3 \leq 5$, use the Kruskal-Wallis Table.
   b. Larger samples use Chi-Square Table with df $= k - 1$.

   Example from formula above, the sample size is appropriate for the Kruskal-Wallis Table.

5. If obtained H value is equal to or less than the previously set level of significance, α, reject H_o in favor of H_1.

In example cited, the obtained value H = 9.76 with n's = 5, 4, 3, and critical probability $< .01$. Reject H_o.

Now calculate the Dunn's Multiple Comparison Test (below) to find any significant differences among the rank means.

Dunn's Multiple Comparison Procedure
Following Kruskal-Wallis Test

Function: When significant results occur in the Kruskal-Wallis test, compute the Dunn's formula to determine which rank means are significantly different . . . compare only 2 ranks at a time. . . . Dunn's test after Kruskal-Wallis is comparable to the Newman-Keuls test after an Analysis of Variance.

$\overline{R}_1$ = mean of group 1 ranks

$\overline{R}_2$ = mean of group 2 ranks (R_3 is group 3 mean, etc.)

$|\overline{R}_1 - \overline{R}_2|$ = absolute value of $\overline{R}_1$ minus $\overline{R}_2$

K = number of groups

N = number of observations in all groups

n_1 = number of observations in group 1

n_2 = number of observations in group 2 (n_3 for group 3)

α = alpha for the Dunn's Test is either .15 or .08 to account for the experimentwise error rate, with .08 being more stringent or conservative.

Z = value found in Table A in Appendix, that is, the Dunn's formula within the first set of parenthesizes is computed and the corresponding Z value (Table A) is located; for example,

$$\left(Z_{(\alpha/[K(K-1)])} \right) = Z_{(.08/3(3-1))} = .0133$$

.0133 = 2.22 Z value which is used to compute the remaining Dunn's formula.

Decision = if formula is true, then means are significantly different.

FORMULA

$$|\overline{R}_1 - \overline{R}_2| \geq \left(Z_{(\alpha/[K(K-1)])} \right) \left(\sqrt{\frac{N(N+1)}{12}} \right) \left(\sqrt{\frac{1}{n_1} + \frac{1}{n_2}} \right)$$

$$|5.2 - 10.5| \geq \left(Z_{.08/3(3-1)} \right) \left(\sqrt{\frac{12(12+1)}{12}} \right) \left(\sqrt{\frac{1}{5} + \frac{1}{4}} \right)$$

$$5.3 \geq (.0133 = Z \text{ of } 2.22) \qquad (3.61) \qquad (.67)$$

$$5.3 \geq 5.37 \quad \text{N. S.}$$

$$(5.2 - 3.3) \geq 5.86 \quad \text{N. S.}$$
$$1.9$$

$$(10.5 - 3.3) \geq 6.08 \quad \text{Significant}$$
$$7.2$$

Differences Among Three Group Means		
5.2	10.5	3.3
		$p < .08$

Musical Example
Kruskal-Wallis One-Way Analysis of Variance

Research Design: Four small independent groups of music students without piano background take class piano. Group 1 receives 80% approval comments from teacher: Group 2 receives 80% negative feedback from disapproving teacher: Group 3 has instruction only; and Group 4 has no contact. A posttest is given to all.

Hypotheses: H_o: There is no difference in scores among the four groups representative population distributions.

H_1: There is a difference in scores among the four groups representative population distributions.

Statistical Test: Kruskal-Wallis One-Way Analysis of Variance compares k independent samples by rank sums.

Level of Significance: α = .05   N = 17 (sum of all n's)

n_1 = 5 n_4 = 3
n_2 = 5 n_5 =
n_3 = 4 n_6 =

Sampling Distribution: Small samples with k (groups) = 3. . . . Number in each group $\leq$ 5, probability found in Kruskal-Wallis Table.

Large samples approximate the chi-square distribution with df = k − 1. Probability found in the Chi-Square Table.

Procedure:

1. Rank all observations for k groups in a single series, assigning ranks from 1 (lowest score) to N (highest).

2. Determine the value of R (sum of ranks) for each of the k groups of ranks.

Example: Kruskal-Wallis Score-and-Rank Table

According to the Four Groups

Group 1		Group 2		Group 3		Group 4		Group 5	
Score	Rank	Score	Rank	Score	Rank	Score	Rank	Score	Rank
98		92		76		65			
89		81		82		70			
75		74		64		43			
85		70		45					
90		57							
sum of ranks . . . R_1 =		R_2 =		R_3 =		R_4 =		R_5 =	
$\bar{R}_1$ =		$\bar{R}_2$ =		$\bar{R}_3$ =		$\bar{R}_4$ =		$\bar{R}_5$ =	

(R = the mean of a group's ranks. R's are used in Dunn's Multiple Comparison Procedure which is done after a Kruskal-Wallis Test

3. Compute the value of H with the Kruskal-Wallis Formula:

$$H = \frac{12}{N\ (N\ +\ 1)}\ \Sigma\ \frac{R^2}{n}\ -\ 3\ (N\ +\ 1)$$

For tied scores use this formula:

$$H = \frac{\frac{12}{N(N+1)} \; \Sigma \; \frac{R^2}{n} \; - \; 3(N+1)}{1 \; - \; \frac{\Sigma T}{N^3 - N}}$$

4. To find statistical significance of obtained H value, use appropriate Table:
   a. Kruskal-Wallis Table if $k = 3$ and no $n > 5$.
   b. Chi-Square Table if larger sample (df $= k - 1$).

   Obtained H = _____   Tabled H = _____   with p = _____

5. Statistical Decision: (If obtained probability is equal to or less than the previously set level of significance, α, reject H_o in favor of H_1).

6. Experimental Decision:

Obtained H = 8.76 Since $k = 4$, use Chi-Square Table, df = 3, tabled value = 7.82 when $\alpha = .05$. Since obtained value is greater than Chi-Square value, $p < .05$, reject H_o. Next compute Dunn's Multiple Comparison Procedure (next page).

Dunn's Multiple Comparison Procedure
Following Kruskal-Wallis Test

Function: When significant results occur in the Kruskal-Wallis test, compute the Dunn's formula to determine which rank means are significantly different . . . compare only 2 ranks at a time. . . . Dunn's test after Kruskal-Wallis is comparable to the Newman-Keuls test after an Analysis of Variance.

KEY TO DUNN'S FORMULA

$\overline{R}_1$ = mean of group 1 ranks

$\overline{R}_2$ = mean of group 2 ranks ($\overline{R}_3$ is group 3 mean, etc.)

$|\overline{R}_1 - \overline{R}_2|$ = absolute value of $\overline{R}_1$ minus $\overline{R}_2$

K = number of groups

N = number of observations in all groups

n_1 = number of observations in group 1

n_2 = number of observations in group 2 (n_3 for group 3)

α = alpha for the Dunn's Test is either <u>.15 or .08</u> to account for the experimentwise error rate, with .08 being more stringent or conservative.

Z = value found in Table A in Appendix, that is, the Dunn's formula within the first set of parenthesizes is computed and the corresponding Z value (Table A) is located: for example,

$$\left(Z_{(\alpha/[K\ (K\ -\ 1)])} \right) = Z_{(.08/3(3\ -\ 1)} = .0133$$

.0133 = 2.22 Z value which is used to compute the remaining Dunn's formula.

Decision = if formula is true, then means are significantly different.

FORMULA

$$|\bar{R}_1 - \bar{R}_2| \geq \left(Z_{(\alpha/[K(K\ -\ 1)])} \right) \left(\sqrt{\frac{N(N\ +\ 1)}{12}} \right) \left(\sqrt{\frac{1}{n_1} + \frac{1}{n_2}} \right)$$

$$|13.6 - 8.9| \geq \left(Z_{.08/[4(4\ -\ 1)]} \right) \left(\sqrt{\frac{17\ (17\ +\ 1)}{12}} \right) \left(\sqrt{\frac{1}{5} + \frac{1}{5}} \right)$$

$$4.7 \qquad \geq \qquad (.0067 = Z\ 2.48) \qquad\qquad (5.05) \qquad\qquad (.63)$$

$$4.7 \qquad \geq \qquad 7.89\ \text{N. S.}$$

$$\geq$$

$$\geq$$

---

1 $-$ 3: (6.6 $\geq$ 8.4)   1 $-$ 4: (9.44 $\geq$ 9.1)*   2 $-$ 3: (1.9 $\geq$ 8.4)   others N. S.

F O R M
Kruskal-Wallis One-Way Analysis of Variance

Research Design

Hypotheses: H_o:

$\qquad$ H_1:

Statistical Test: Kruskal-Wallis One-Way Analysis of Variance compares k independent samples by rank sums.

$N = \underline{\hspace{2cm}}$ (sum of all n's)

Level of Significance: $\alpha = .\underline{\hspace{2cm}}$

$\qquad n_1 = \underline{\hspace{2cm}} \qquad n_4 = \underline{\hspace{2cm}}$

$\qquad\qquad k = \underline{\hspace{2cm}}$

$\qquad n_2 = \underline{\hspace{2cm}} \qquad n_5 = \underline{\hspace{2cm}}$

$\qquad n_3 = \underline{\hspace{2cm}} \qquad n_6 = \underline{\hspace{2cm}}$

Sampling Distribution: Small samples with k (groups) = 3 . . . number in each group $\leq$ 5, probability found in Kruskal-Wallis Table.

Large samples approximate the chi-square distribution with df = $k - 1$ . . . . Probability found in the Chi-Square Table.

Procedure

1. Rank all the observations for k groups in a single series, assigning ranks from 1 (lowest score) to N (highest).
2. Determine the value of R (sum of ranks) for each of the k groups of ranks.

Kruskal-Wallis Score and Rank Table
According to Groups

Group 1 Score Rank	Group 2 Score Rank	Group 3 Score Rank	Group 4 Score Rank	Group 5 Score Rank
Sum of Ranks $R_1 =$ ____	$R_2 =$ ____	$R_3 =$ ____	$R_4 =$ ____	$R_5 =$ ____
$\overline{R}_1 =$	$\overline{R}_2 =$	$\overline{R}_3 =$	$\overline{R}_4 =$	$\overline{R}_5 =$

($\overline{R} =$ the mean of a group's ranks. $\overline{R}$'s are used in Dunn's Multiple Comparison Procedure which is done after a Kruskal-Wallis Test).

3. Compute the value of H with the Kruskal-Wallis Formula:

$$H = \frac{12}{N(N+1)} \;\; \Sigma \frac{R^2}{n} \; - 3(N+1)$$

For tied scores use this formula:

$$H = \frac{\dfrac{12}{N(N+1)} \;\; \Sigma \dfrac{R^2}{n} - 3(N+1)}{1 - \dfrac{\Sigma T}{N^3 - N}}$$

4. To find statistical significance of obtained H value, use appropriate Table:
   a. Kruskal-Wallis Table if $k = 3$ and no $n > 5$.
   b. Chi-Square Table if larger sample. df $= k - 1$.

   Obtained H = _____

   Tabled H = _____with p = _____

5. Statistical Decision: (If obtained probability is equal to or less than the previously set level of significance, α, reject H_0 in favor of H_1.)

6. Experimental Decision: _____

FORM
Dunn's Multiple Comparison Procedure
Following Kruskal-Wallis Test

Function: When significant results occur in the Kruskal-Wallis test, compute the Dunn's formula to determine which rank means are significantly different . . . compare only 2 ranks at a time. . . . Dunn's test after Kruskal-Wallis is comparable to the Newman-Keuls test after an Analysis of Variance.

KEY TO DUNN'S FORMULA

$\overline{R}_1$ = mean of group 1 ranks

$\overline{R}_2$ = mean of group 2 ranks (R_3 is group 3 mean, etc.)

$| \overline{R}_1 - \overline{R}_2 |$ = absolute value of $\overline{R}_1$ minus $\overline{R}_2$

K = number of groups

N = number of observations in all groups

n_1 = number of observations in group 1

n_2 = number of observations in group 2 (n_3 for group 3)

α = alpha for the Dunn's Test is either .15 or .08 to account for the experimentwise error rate, with .08 being more stringent or conservative.

Z = value found in Table A in Appendix, that is, the Dunn's formula within the first set of parenthesize is computed and the corresponding Z value (Table A) is located; for example,

$$\left(Z_{(\alpha/[K(K-1)])} \right) = Z_{(.08/3(3-1))} = .0133$$
.0133 = 2.22 Z value which is used to compute the remaining Dunn's formula.

Decision = if formula is true, then means are significantly different.

$$| \ \overline{R}_1 \ - \ \overline{R}_2 \ | \ \geq \ \left(Z_{(\alpha/[K(K \ - \ 1)] \ )} \right) \ \left(\sqrt{\frac{N(N \ + \ 1)}{12}} \right) \ \left(\sqrt{\frac{1}{n_1} \ + \ \frac{1}{n_2}} \right)$$

$$\geq$$

$$\geq$$

$$\geq$$

$$\geq$$

$$\geq$$

---

t Test

Rationale and Assumptions: t test is the parametric test for comparing the means of samples from populations. . . . Samples can be independent or related. . . . Samples may be equal or unequal in size. . . . Generally, the level of measurement is interval.

Three Assumptions:

1. Samples are drawn from normally distributed populations or from populations with known distributions.
2. Population variances (σ^2) are the same (homogeneous).
3. At least interval measurement is used.

Addition assumptions are usually appropriate for the practical use of the "robust" t test:

1. N is large (30 or more).
2. Two-tailed test is used.
3. Equal sample sizes.

Hypotheses: H_o: The mean of one group comes from the same population as the mean of the other group.

H_1: the means of both groups come from different population distributions.

Level of Significance: usually α = .05 or .01.

The Procedures are carefully described on the following pages with the appropriate formulas.

A t test compares the means of two groups taking into account the variances.

If you are working with a calculator, the **Form B** formula for the standard deviation will be handy. Remember that the variance is the standard deviation squared when you are working with the t tests.

If you are not working with a calculator, then **Form A** might be easier to use.

Process for Selecting t Test:

1. Are the samples independent or dependent?
*2. Are the sample sizes equal (n_1 = n_2) or unequal (n_1 ≠ n_2)?

*For independent samples only. Obviously N_1 must equal N_2 in dependent samples.

3. Are the variances equal ($s_1^2 = s_2^2$) or unequal ($s_1^2 \neq s_2^2$)?

4. After determining the above three steps see t test chart to determine the appropriate t test.

t Test Chart

	$n_1 = n_2$		$n_1 \neq n_2$	
	$s_1^2 = s_2^2$	$s_1^2 \neq s_2^2$	$s_1^2 = s_2^2$	$s_1^2 \neq s_2^2$
Independent	C	D	E*, F	G*, H
Dependent	A, B	A, B	A, B	A, B

*More "conservative" of the two tests, i.e., the test with which it is harder to reject the H_o.

The capital letters refer to formulas given on the following pages.

Note: Formulas E, F, G, and H may also be used when $n_1 = n_2$.

t Test Formulas:

A: $$t = \frac{\overline{d} - d_o}{s_d / \sqrt{n}} \qquad \text{where} \qquad s_d = \sqrt{\frac{n(\Sigma di^2) - (\Sigma di)^2}{(n)(n-1)}}$$

$\overline{d}$ = mean of difference scores

n = number of paired observations

d_o = expected difference (usually zero)

df = $n - 1$

B: $$t = \frac{\Sigma d}{\sqrt{\dfrac{n \, \Sigma \, d^2 - (\Sigma d)^2}{n - 1}}}$$

C: $$t = \frac{\overline{X}_1 - \overline{X}_2 - 0}{\sqrt{\dfrac{s_1^2 + s_2^2}{n}}} \qquad \begin{array}{l} n_1 = n_2 \\[6pt] s_1^2 = s_2^2 \end{array}$$

df = $2(n-1)$

n = number of observations in one group

D: $$t = \frac{\overline{X}_1 - \overline{X}_2}{\sqrt{\dfrac{s_1^2 + s_2^2}{n}}} \qquad \begin{array}{l} n_1 = n_2 \\[6pt] s_1^2 \neq s_2^2 \end{array}$$

df = $n - 1$

n = number of observations in one group

E:

$n_1 \neq n_2$

$s_1^2 = s_2^2$

$$t = \frac{\overline{X}_1 - \overline{X}_2}{\sqrt{\left[\dfrac{(n_1 - 1)\,s_1^2 + (n_2 - 1)\,s_2^2}{(n_1 - 1) + (n_2 - 1)}\right]\left(\dfrac{n_1 + n_2}{n_1\,n_2}\right)}}$$

$df = (n_1 - 1) + (n_2 - 1)$

F:

$n_1 = n_2$

$s_1^2 \neq s_2^2$

$$\frac{\overline{X}_1 - \overline{X}_2}{Sp\sqrt{\dfrac{1}{n_1} + \dfrac{1}{n_2}}} = t$$

Pooled

$$\text{Variance} = Sp = \sqrt{\left(\frac{(n_1 - 1)\,s_1^2 + (n_2 - 1)\,s_2^2}{n_1 + n_2 - 2}\right)}$$

$df = n_1 + n_2 - 2$

G:

$n_1 \neq n_2$

$s_1^2 \neq s_2^2$

$$t = \frac{\overline{X}_1 - \overline{X}_2}{\sqrt{\left(\dfrac{s_1^2}{n_1}\right) + \left(\dfrac{s_2^2}{n_2}\right)}}$$

$$df = \frac{\left(\dfrac{s_1^2}{n_1} + \dfrac{s_2^2}{n_2}\right)^2}{\left[\dfrac{(s_1^2 / n_1)^2}{(n_1 - 1)} + \dfrac{(s_2^2 / n_2)^2}{(n_2 - 1)}\right]}$$

H:

$n_1 \neq n_2$

$s_1^2 \neq s_2^2$

$$t = \frac{\overline{X}_1 - \overline{X}_2}{\sqrt{\dfrac{s_1^2}{n_1} + \dfrac{s_2^2}{n_2}}}$$

$df = (n_1 - 1) + (n_2 - 1)$

Test For Equality of Variances: Used in determining which *t* formula to use for independent samples.

$$F = \frac{s^2 \ (largest)}{s^2 \ (smallest)}$$

In order to find the proper value in an F table use the corresponding degrees of freedom values as shown below:

$$F = \frac{df \ associated \ with \ largest \ s^2}{df \ associated \ with \ smallest \ s^2}$$

H_o: $s_1^2 = s_2^2$ at alpha = .05. If the obtained value from the formula at the top of this page is larger than the critical value of F for its associated degrees of freedom, then conclude $s_1^2 \neq s_2^2$.

For example, if the s^2 of group 1 is 4.56 and the variance (s^2) of group 2 is 2.94, then substituting these values

$$\frac{4.56}{2.94} = 1.55.$$

If $n_1 = 31$ and $n_2 = 25$, then df = 30, 24. The critical F value for these values is 1.94. As the obtained F of 1.55 is less than the critical value it is concluded that the variances are equal.

Problem: Group 1 (n = 21) and group 2 (n = 16) have variances of 17.6 and 24.8 respectively. Does one conclude that the n's are equal or unequal?

> The Obtained F Ratio is 1.41. As the Critical Value of F is 2.27, Conclude that the Variances Are Equal.

Compute a t test for dependent samples on the following data. Work the problem twice, once with Form A, and once with Form B.

Subject	Score A	Score B	d	d²
n1	15	14		
n2	16	14		
n3	14	11		
n4	18	14		
n5	17	12		
n6	16	10		
n7	19	12		
n8	17	9		
n9	22	13		

H_o: There is no difference between subjects' A scores and B scores.

$\Sigma d = 45$

$\Sigma d^2 = 285$

$\overline{d} = 5$

$t = 5.478$ (A)

$t = 5.476$ (B)

$n = 9$

When $\alpha = .05$ and df $= 8$, the critical value for $\underline{t} = 2.306$ *

Decision: Since the obtained $\underline{t}$ (5.478) is larger than the critical value of $\underline{t}$ (2.306), reject H_o.

*(See Table G in Appendix)

Given two independent samples with the following scores, determine which t formula to use, and compute it.

Group 1	Group 2
48	48
52	51
56	54
60	57
64	60
68	63
72	66
76	69
80	72
84	75

Formula C

$$F_{9,9} = \frac{s_1^2}{s_2^2} = \frac{146.667}{82.5} = 1.7778 \ (C\ V = 3.18)$$

$t = .94$

$df = 18$

Critical value of $\underline{t} = 2.101$

$\Sigma X_1 = 660$

$\Sigma X_1^2 = 44,880$

$\alpha = .05$

$\Sigma X_2 = 615$

$\Sigma X_2^2 = 38,565$

Decision: Fail to reject H_o

Given two independent samples with the following scores, determine which t formula to use, and compute t.

Group 1	Group 2
9	1
10	9
11	21
12	30
13	8
14	5
15	17
16	24

Formula D

$$\cdot F_{7,7} = \frac{s_2^2}{s_1^2} = \frac{103.411}{6} = 17.2352$$

$$(C\ V = 3.79)$$

$\Sigma X_1 = 100$ $\Sigma X_2 = 115$ $\overline{X}_1 = 12.5$

$\Sigma X_1^2 = 1{,}292$ $\Sigma X_2^2 = 2377$ $\overline{X}_2 = 14.375$

$s_1^2 = 6$ $s_2^2 = 103.411$

$t = .5070$ Critical $\underline{t} = 2.365$ $\alpha = .05$

$df = 7$ Decision: Fail to reject H_o

Given two independent samples with the following scores, determine which t formula to use, and compute t.

Group 1	Group 2
16	24
17	25
17	26
18	27
18	28
19	29
19	30
20	31
21	32
21	
22	
22	
23	
23	
24	

Formula E or F

$$F_{8,14} = \frac{s_2^2}{s_1^2} = \frac{7.5}{6.2857} = 1.1932$$

$\Sigma X_1 = 300$ $n_1 = 15$

$\Sigma X_1^2 = 6088$ $n_2 = 9$

$\Sigma X_2 = 252$ $\overline{X}_1 = 20$

$\Sigma X_2^2 = 7116$ $\overline{X}_2 = 28$

$t_{(E)} = 7.3153$ $t_{(F)} = 7.316$

$df = 22$ $df = 22$

Critical $\underline{t} = 2.074$ with $\alpha = .05$ & $df = 22$ Decision: Reject H_o

Given two independent samples with the following scores, determine which t formula to use, and compute t.

Group 1	Group 2
5	0
6	2
7	4
7	6
8	8
8	10
9	12
9	14
10	16
11	18
	20
	22

Formula G or H

$$F_{11,19} = \frac{s_2^2}{s_1^2} = \frac{52}{3.333} = 15.602 \ (C V = 3.14) \ s_1^2 \neq s_2^2$$

$\Sigma X_1 = 80 \qquad \Sigma X_2 = 132$

$\Sigma X_1^2 = 670 \qquad \Sigma X_2^2 = 2024$

$t_{(G)} = 1.389 \qquad\qquad t_{(H)} = 1.389$

$df = 13 \qquad\qquad\qquad df = 20$

$2.160 = $ Critical values of $\underline{t} = 2.086 \qquad \alpha = .05$

Decision: Fail to reject H_o

The following summarized data describe the heights of boys and girls in a 7th grade band. State and test an appropriate null hypothesis.

Boys	Girls
$\overline{X} = 60$	$\overline{X} = 75$
$s = 5.3$	$s = 6.1$
$n = 14$	$n = 11$

H_0: There is no difference between the average height of boys and girls in the seventh grade class.

Formula E or F.

$$n_1 \neq n_2 \qquad s_1^2 = s_2^2$$

$$F_{10,13} = \frac{37.21}{28.09} = 1.32 \qquad (C\ V\ =\ 2.67)$$

$$t_{(E)} = 6.5764$$

$$df = 23$$

α = .05, Critical Value (C V) of $\underline{t}$ for α = .05 with df = 23 is 2.069.

As our obtained t (6.5764) is greater than the critical value H_0 is rejected. It is concluded that there is a significant difference in the height of boys and girls in the seventh grade band.

The following data describe the scores of two choruses on sight-singing at a state music contest. State and test an appropriate hypothesis.

Group A	Group B
$\overline{X}$ = 76	$\overline{X}$ = 81
s = 3.4	s = 5.2
n = 36	n = 25

H_0: There is no difference in performance between the two choruses.

Formula G or H.

$$n_1 \neq n_2 \qquad s_1^2 \neq s_2^2$$

$$F_{24,35} = \frac{s_2^2}{s_1^2} = \frac{27.04}{11.56} = 2.3391 \qquad (C\ V\ =\ 1.89)$$

$$t_{(H)} = 4.2233$$

$$df = 59$$

α = .05; the C V of t for α = .05
with df = 59 is 1.96.

As the obtained value of t (6.5764) is greater than the critical value (1.96) the null hypothesis is rejected. It is concluded that there is a significant difference between the scores earned by the two choruses.

F O R M

t test for matched or dependent groups

Experiment: _____ Date: _____

X_1: _____

X_2: _____

D = algebraic difference between paired scores $(X_1 - X_2)$ n = no. pairs

$H_o = u_D = 0$ $H_1 = u_D = 0$ α = _____ $df = n - 1$ = _____

check: $\Sigma X_1 - \Sigma X_2 = \Sigma D$ _____ − _____ = _____

$$t = \frac{M - u}{D \quad D} = \frac{\Sigma D}{} =$$

$$= \sqrt{\frac{s^2_D}{n}} = \sqrt{\frac{n \, \Sigma D^2 - (\Sigma D)^2}{n - 1}} =$$

t = _____ , df = _____ , p = _____

Decision: _____

S. No.	X_1	X_2	D	D^2
1				
2				
3				
4				
5				
6				
7				
8				
9				
10				
11				
12				
13				
14				
15				
16				
17				
18				
19				
20				
21				
22				
23				
24				
25				

F O R M

Date :

Experiment:

t test, independent samples, $n_1 =$

X_1 : X_2 :

1. Test for heterogeneity of population variances $(H_o : \sigma_1^2 = \sigma_2^2, H_1 : \sigma_1^2 \neq \sigma_2^2 ; \alpha = \underline{\quad})$

$$s_1^2 = \frac{n\Sigma X^2 - (\Sigma X)^2}{n_1 (n_1 - 1)} =$$

$$s_2^2 = \frac{n\Sigma X^2 - (\Sigma X)^2}{n_2 (n_2 - 1)} =$$

$$F = \frac{\text{larger } S^2}{\text{smaller } S^2} =$$

$df's = n - 1 =$

$p =$

Decision

2. Test for difference between population means $(H_o : \mu_1 = \mu_2 ; H_1 : \mu_1 \neq \mu_2 ; \alpha =$

2.1 Population variances homogeneous $(\sigma_1^2 = \sigma_1^2)$

$$t = \frac{M_1 - M_2}{\sqrt{\dfrac{S_1^2 + S_2^2}{n}}}$$

$df = 2(n - 1) =$

$p =$

Decision =

2.2 Population variances heterogeneous $(\sigma_1^2 \neq \sigma_2^2)$

exactly as above (2.1), or, for conservative test, simply refer t value

to tables with df = n−1

$df =$ p Decision

Data S no.	X_1	X_2
1		
2		
3		
4		
5		
6		
7		
8		
9		
10		
11		
12		
13		
14		
15		
16		
17		
18		
19		
20		
ΣX		
ΣX^2		
M		

F O R M

t test, independent samples, $n_1 \neq n_2$

Experiment

$X_1 : =$

$X_2 : =$

1. Test for heterogeneity of population variances $\left(H_o : \sigma_1^2 = \sigma_2^2 , H_1 : \sigma_1^2 \neq \sigma_2^2 \quad \alpha = \quad\right)$

$$S_1^{\,2} = \frac{n_1 \Sigma X_1^{\,2} - (\Sigma X)^2}{n_1 (n_1 - 1)} = \qquad = \qquad F = \frac{\text{larger } S^2}{\text{smaller } S^2} = \qquad =$$

$$S_2^{\,2} = \frac{n_2 \Sigma X^2 - (\Sigma X)^2}{} = \qquad$$

$$df = (n_1 - 1) , (n_2 - 1) , = \underline{\qquad}$$

$$p = \qquad \text{Decision} \underline{\qquad}$$

2. Test for differences between population means $\left(H_o : \mu_1 = \mu_2 \quad \mu_1 \neq \mu_2 \quad \alpha = \right)$

2.1 Population variance homogeneous $\left(\sigma_1^{\,2} = \sigma_2^{\,2}\right)$

$$t = \frac{M_1 - M_2}{\sqrt{\left[\dfrac{(n_1 - 1)S_1^{\,2} + (n_2 - 1)S_2^{\,2}}{(n_1 - 1) + (n_2 - 1)}\right]\left(\dfrac{n_1 + n_2}{n_1 n_2}\right)}}$$

$$df = (n_1 - 1) + (n_2 - 1) = \qquad p = \qquad \text{Decision:} \underline{\qquad}$$

2.2 Population variances heterogeneous $\left(\sigma_1^{\,2} \neq \sigma_2^{\,2}\right)$

$$t = \frac{M_1 - M_2}{\sqrt{\dfrac{S_1^{\,2}}{n_1} + \dfrac{S_2^{\,2}}{n_2}}} = \qquad = \qquad \text{followed by Cochran's}$$

$$t^1 = \frac{t_1\left(\dfrac{S_1^{\,2}}{n_1}\right) + t_2\left(\dfrac{S_2^{\,2}}{n_2}\right)}{\left(\dfrac{S_1^{\,2}}{n_1}\right) + \left(\dfrac{S_2^{\,2}}{n_2}\right)} = \qquad \text{Decision} \underline{\qquad}$$

Data

S no.	X_1	X_2
1		
2		
3		
4		
5		
6		
7		
8		
9		
10		
11		
12		
13		
14		
15		
16		
17		
18		
19		
20		
21		
22		
$\sum\limits^{n} X$		
$\sum\limits^{n} X^2$		
M		

One-Way Analysis of Variance (ANOVA)
F Test

Rationale and Assumptions: The F test is a parametric test for comparing the means/variances among samples drawn from theoretical populations. . . . The F test is a theoretical probability distribution which is stated in the form of a ratio. . . . The ratio of the between mean sum of squares over the within mean sum of squares. . . . Three or more samples.

Assumptions of the F Test:

1. Samples drawn from normally distributed populations.
2. Random and independent selection of samples.
3. Population variances are equal or homogeneous.
4. At least interval measurement is required.
5. The means of the normally distributed populations must be linear combinations of effects due to columns and/or rows, i.e., the effects must be additive.

These assumptions are all theoretical and sometimes difficult to verify. Often one or more is not met and the test is jeopardized. But due to the strength or "robustness" of the F test, the ANOVA is usually appropriate if the following conditions are met:

1. N is large (30 or more).
2. Two-tailed test is used.
3. Equal sample sizes.

Hypotheses: H_o: Variance of one group equals the variance of the other group. $\sigma_1^2 = \sigma_1^2$

H_1: Variances are not equal. $\sigma_1^2 \neq \sigma_2^2$

Level of Significance: usually $\alpha = .05$.

Procedure:

1. Place scores in data table and calculate:
    a. Sum of scores for each column: ΣX.
    b. Sum of squared scores for each column: ΣX^2.
    c. Sum of scores squared for each column: $(\Sigma X)^2$.
    d. Mean of each group: $\overline{X}$ or $\overline{A}$.
2. Calculate necessary terms:
    a. Sum the sum of all the scores $\overset{a}{\Sigma}\overset{s}{\Sigma}X$.
    b. Sum the sum of all the squares $\overset{a}{\Sigma}\overset{s}{\Sigma}X^2$.
    c. Sum the sum of all the scores squared $\overset{a}{\Sigma}(\overset{s}{\Sigma}X)^2$.
    d. Do 2(c) and divide by number of subjects in that group.

    $$\frac{\overset{a}{\Sigma}(\overset{s}{\Sigma}X)^2}{s}$$

    e. Sum all the scores, then square $(\overset{a}{\Sigma}\overset{s}{\Sigma}X)^2$.

f. Do 2(e) and divide by the total number of subjects.

$$\frac{(\overset{a}{\Sigma}\overset{s}{\Sigma}X)^2}{as}$$

g. Obtain the Matrix Mean by summing all the means and divide by number of groups (the mean of the means)

$$\overline{M} = \frac{\Sigma(\overline{A}a)}{a}$$

3. Calculate the Sum of Squares formulas with necessary terms and fill in the ANOVA Table.
Sum of Squares Formula *between* groups:

$$ss_A = \frac{\overset{a}{\Sigma}\,(\overset{s}{\Sigma}X)}{s} - \frac{(\overset{a}{\Sigma}\overset{s}{\Sigma}X)^2}{as}$$

Sum of Squares Formula *within* groups:

$$ss_{s(A)} = \overset{a}{\Sigma}\overset{s}{\Sigma}X^2 - \frac{\overset{a}{\Sigma}(\overset{s}{\Sigma}X)^2}{s}$$

Total Sum of Squares:

$$ss_{TOT} = \overset{a}{\Sigma}\overset{s}{\Sigma}X^2 - \frac{(\overset{a}{\Sigma}\overset{s}{\Sigma}X)^2}{as}$$

4. Calculate the df (degrees of freedom) for the three sources in the ANOVA Table.

5. Calculate the Mean Sum of Squares by dividing the Sum of Squares by the degrees of freedom for each source.

6. To find the F ratio, divide the *between* Mean Sum of Squares by the *within* Sum of Squares:

$$\frac{s_A^{\,2}}{s_{s(A)}^{\,2}}$$

7. Check the F Table for the critical value, remember the level of alpha (α) set and the df for both groups, df $= n - 1$.

8. If the obtained F is equal to or *more* than the critical value, reject H_o.

9. To determine which means are significantly different, calculate a *t* test after the F test. Precautions should be taken in not doing several *t* tests on the same data. The best alternative is the Studentized Range Statistic (See Winer, p. 185ff.).

Analysis of Variance
Data Table

Musical Example

	A_1 (s = 25)	A_2 (s = 25)	A_3 (s = 25)	A_4 (s =)
	16	16	14	
	12	14	12	
	8	12	10	
	10	10	9	
	12	13	8	
	14	14	10	
	14	12	12	
	14	13	11	
	15	14	13	
	8	10	8	
	10	10	11	
	11	12	7	
	12	13	6	
	7	10	5	
	6	12	9	
	8	10	10	
	12	12	5	
	7	11	6	
	6	12	4	
	5	13	9	
	8	10	11	
	7	15	7	
	11	12	8	
	10	11	9	
	9	10	10	

Study: Effective methods to improve articulaton. Seventy-five undergraduates in music chosen randomly. Three equal sized groups perform articulation exercise. All study over 10 week period and take posttest.

A_1 = teacher comments
A_2 = teacher model
A_3 = no contact control group
A_4 =

a = # of Groups   3
s = # of Subjects   25
as = # Total   75

	A_1	A_2	A_3		
ΣX	252	301	224	→	$\overset{a\ s}{\Sigma\Sigma} X$ 777
ΣX^2	2,768	3,695	2,168	→	$\overset{a\ s}{\Sigma\Sigma} X^2$ 8,631
$(\Sigma X)^2$	63,504	90,601	50,176	→	$\overset{a\ \ s}{\Sigma (\Sigma X)^2}$ 204,281
A_a	10.08	12.04	8.96		$\dfrac{\overset{a\ \ s}{\Sigma (\Sigma X)^2}}{s}$ 8,171.24
					$\overset{a\ s}{(\Sigma\Sigma X)^2}$ 603,729
					$\dfrac{\overset{a\ s}{(\Sigma\Sigma X)^2}}{as}$ 8,049.72
					$\overline{M}$ 10.36

$$F = \frac{\text{mean sum of square between groups}}{\text{mean sum of square within groups}}$$

$$F = \frac{\text{ss between/df}}{\text{ss within/df}}$$

Check: is

$$\overset{a\ s}{\Sigma\Sigma} X^2 > \frac{\overset{a\ \ s}{\Sigma (\Sigma X)^2}}{s} > \frac{\overset{a\ s}{(\Sigma\Sigma X)^2}}{as} \quad ?$$

$$8,631 > 8,171 > 8,049$$

FORM

Analysis of Variance "F" Table

Source	SS	df	$S^2 = MS$	F
S_A^2 (between)	121.52	$(a-1)$ 2	60.76	9.515
$S_{S(A)}^2$ (within)	459.76	$(as-a)$ 72	6.386	/
S^2 TOTAL	581.28	$(as-1)$ 74	/	/

SUM OF SQUARES

$$SS_A = \overset{a}{\underset{}{\Sigma}}\ \overset{s}{\underset{}{\frac{(\Sigma X)^2}{s}}} - \frac{(\Sigma\Sigma X)^2}{as} = \underline{8{,}171.24} - \underline{8{,}049.72} = 121{:}52$$

$$SS_{S(A)} = \overset{as}{\underset{}{\Sigma\Sigma}} X^2 - \frac{\overset{as}{\underset{}{\Sigma}}(\Sigma X)^2}{s} = \underline{8{,}631} - \underline{8{,}171.24} = 459.76$$

$$SS_{TOTAL} = \overset{as}{\underset{}{\Sigma\Sigma}} X^2 - \frac{(\Sigma\Sigma X)^2}{as} = \underline{8{,}631} - \underline{8{,}049.72} = 581.28$$

MEAN SQ $= S^2$

$$S_A^2 = \frac{SS\ between}{a-1} = \frac{121.52}{2} = \underline{60.76}$$

$$S_{S(A)}^2 = \frac{SS\ within}{as-a} = \frac{459.72}{72} = \underline{6.386}$$

$H_o: \sigma_\mu^2 = 0$

Obtained $F = \dfrac{S_A^2}{S_{S(A)}^2} = \dfrac{60.76}{6.386} = 9.515$

$H_1: \sigma_\mu^2 > 0$

See "F" Table for Critical F Value, $F = 3.15$

$\alpha = .05$

$df = \dfrac{2}{(a-1)}, \dfrac{72}{(as-a)}$

Conclusion: (If obtained value is *more* than critical value, reject H_o)

Decision: $p < .05$ reject H_o _____

To determine any significant difference between the means after obtaining a significant F value, use a Multiple-Range Test, such as the Newman-Keuls Test. See next page.

Newman-Keuls Multiple Comparison Procedure
Example

Tests: After significant F test, use Newman-Keuls test to determine significance between means.

Example: 3 means are ordered (1) 8.96 (2) 10.08 (3) 12.04

Denominator from F ratio used in this formula:

($S^2_{S(D)}$ taken from F table, n = number in one group)

$$s_{\overline{M}} = \sqrt{\frac{S^2_{S(D)}}{n}} \qquad s_{\overline{M}} = \sqrt{\frac{6.386}{25}}$$

$$= .505$$

Knowing df = 72, α = .05 and there are 3 means being compared, look at Table J in the Appendix, Studentized Range Statistic. Taking a modest df = 60, the .95 values are (2) 2.83 and (3) 3.40.

Multiply $S_{\overline{M}}$ times tabled values:
$$(2.83)(.505) = 1.429$$
$$(3.40)(.505) = 1.717$$

$$(1) - (2) = (8.96) - (10.08) = 1.12 \text{ N.S.*}$$

Subtract means from each other:

$$(2) - (3) = (10.08) - (12.04) = 1.96**$$

$$(1) - (3) = (8.96) - (12.04) = 3.08**$$

When number of steps between means is two, difference must be 1.429 to be significant at α = .05. When there are three steps between means, difference must be 1.717 to be significant. Assuming df = 60.

Common way to show results is to arrange means from small to large and underline means which are not significantly different:

<u>8.96   10.08</u>   12.04

*N.S. means no significance.

**means significance.

Musical Example

Analysis of Variance
Data Table

	A_1 (s = 10)	A_2 (s = 10)	A_3 (s = 10)	A_4 (s =)			
	4	5	2				
	2	6	3				
	3	5	2				
	1	4	2				
	2	4	1				
	3	5	1				
	2	4	2				
	4	6	3				
	3	6	2				
	3	5	2				
ΣX				$\rightarrow$	$\overset{a\ s}{\Sigma\Sigma}\ X$	
ΣX^2				$\rightarrow$	$\overset{a\ s}{\Sigma\Sigma}\ X^2$	
$(\Sigma X)^2$				$\rightarrow$	$\overset{a\ \ s}{\Sigma}\ (\Sigma\ X)^2$	
$\overline{A}_a$					$\overset{a\ \ s}{\Sigma}\ \dfrac{(\Sigma\ X)^2}{s}$	
					$\overset{a\ s}{(\Sigma\Sigma\ X)^2}$	
					$\dfrac{\overset{a\ s}{(\Sigma\Sigma\ X)^2}}{as}$	
					$\overline{M}$	

Study: Distraction during practice time. 30 high school band students record number of distractions in 1/2 hour of practice time. Data collected after one semester of the treatments.

A_1 = sensitized by teacher

A_2 = no contact control

A_3 = use tape recorder

A_4 = (fabricated data)

a = # of Groups_____

s = # of Subjects_____

as = # Total_____

$F = \dfrac{\text{mean sum of square between groups}}{\text{mean sum of square within groups}}$

$F = \dfrac{\text{ss between/df}}{\text{ss within/df}}$

Check: is

$\overset{a\ s}{\Sigma\Sigma}\ X^2 > \overset{a\ \ s}{\Sigma}\ \dfrac{(\Sigma X)^2}{s} > \dfrac{\overset{a\ s}{(\Sigma\Sigma\ X)^2}}{a\,s}$?

_____ > _____ > _____

97

FORM

Analysis of Variance "F" Table

Source	SS	df	S^2 = MS	F
S_A^2 (between)		$(a - 1)$		
$S_{S(A)}^2$ (within)		$(as - a)$		
S^2 TOTAL		$(as - 1)$		

SUMS OF SQUARES

$$SS_A = \overset{a}{\underset{}{\Sigma}} \frac{\overset{s}{(\Sigma X)^2}}{s} - \frac{\overset{a\,s}{(\Sigma\Sigma X)^2}}{a\,s} = \underline{\hspace{5cm}} - \underline{\hspace{5cm}} =$$

$$SS_{S(A)} = \overset{a s}{\Sigma\Sigma X^2} - \frac{\overset{a\,s}{\Sigma(\Sigma X)^2}}{s} = \underline{\hspace{5cm}} - \underline{\hspace{5cm}} =$$

$$SS_{TOTAL} = \overset{a\,s}{\Sigma\Sigma} X^2 - \frac{\overset{a\,s}{(\Sigma\Sigma X)^2}}{a\,s} = \underline{\hspace{5cm}} - \underline{\hspace{5cm}} =$$

MEAN SQ = S^2

$$S_A^2 = \frac{SS\ between}{a - 1} = \underline{\hspace{6cm}} =$$

$$S_{S(A)}^2 = \frac{SS\ within}{as - a} = \underline{\hspace{6cm}} =$$

H_o: $\sigma_\mu^2 = 0$

H_1: $\sigma_\mu^2 > 0$

$\alpha = .05$

Obtained F $= \dfrac{S_A^2}{S_{S(A)}^2} = \underline{\hspace{4cm}} =$

See "F" Table for Critical F Value, F = _____

$$df = \frac{}{(a - 1)}\,,\,\frac{}{(as - a)}$$

Conclusion: (If obtained value is *more* than critical value, reject H_o)

Decision: _____

- -

<u>t</u> test-after-F test: Appropriate in deciding difference between two group means. Use t formula and t table for critical value when df = as − 2 = _____.

$$t = \frac{\bar{A}_1 - \bar{A}_2}{\sqrt{2 S_{S(A)}^2 /n}}$$

Obtained F = 36.77   Significant

Newman-Keuls Multiple Comparison Procedure
Following ANOVA

Tests: After significant F test, use Newman-Keuls to test any significant differences between means.

Necessary Terms: α = . _____   df = _____   n = _____ (one group)

$$s_{\overline{M}} = \sqrt{\frac{S^2{}_{S(D)}}{n}} \qquad \text{and} \qquad \overline{A}_1 - \overline{A}_2 = q\,(s_{\overline{M}})$$

Formula: When $S^2{}_{S(D)}$ = within variance found in MS column of F table. $S^2{}_{S(D)}$ is the denominator in an F ratio.

$\overline{A}$ = mean of group A.

q = tabled value in Table J in the Appendix, the Studentized Range Statistic. First find df in left column, then decide .95 or .99 significance level, then the number of steps between ordered means. Multiply q times $S_{\overline{M}}$ and then subtract the two means. When difference between two means is more than q times $S_{\overline{M}}$ product, difference is significant.

Compute data:

Results:

2.0	2.7	5.0

N.S.

FORM
Analysis of Variance
Data Table

	A_1 (s =)	A_2 (s =)	A_3 (s =)	A_4 (s =)
ΣX				
ΣX^2				
$(\Sigma X)^2$				
$\overline{A}_a$				

Study: _____

_____

_____

_____

_____

_____

_____

_____

_____

$A_1 =$

$A_2 =$

$A_3 =$

$A_4 =$

a = # of Groups _____

s = # of Subjects _____

as = # Total _____

$\overset{a\ s}{\Sigma\Sigma} X$	
$\overset{a\ s}{\Sigma\Sigma} X^2$	
$\overset{a\ \ s}{\Sigma(\Sigma X)^2}$	
$\overset{a\ \ \ s}{\Sigma} \dfrac{(\Sigma X)^2}{s}$	
$(\overset{a\ s}{\Sigma\Sigma} X)^2$	
$\dfrac{(\overset{a\ s}{\Sigma\Sigma} X)^2}{as}$	
$\overline{M}$	

$F = \dfrac{\text{mean sum of squares between groups}}{\text{mean sum of squares within groups}}$

$F = \dfrac{\text{ss between/df}}{\text{ss within/df}}$

Check: is

$\overset{a\ s}{\Sigma\Sigma} X^2 > \overset{a\ \ s}{\Sigma} \dfrac{(\Sigma X)^2}{s} > \dfrac{(\overset{as}{\Sigma\Sigma} X)^2}{as}$?

_____ > _____ > _____

Analysis of Variance "F" Table

Source	SS	df	S^2 = MS	F
$S_A{}^2$ (between)		$(a - 1)$		
$S_{S(A)}{}^2$ (within)		$(as - a)$		
S^2 TOTAL		$(as - 1)$		

SUMS OF SQUARES

$$SS_A = \overset{a}{\underset{}{\Sigma}} \frac{(\overset{s}{\Sigma}X)^2}{s} - \frac{(\overset{a}{\Sigma}\overset{s}{\Sigma}X)^2}{as} = \underline{\hspace{4cm}} - \underline{\hspace{4cm}} =$$

$$SS_{S(A)} = \overset{a\,s}{\Sigma\Sigma}X^2 - \frac{\overset{a}{\Sigma}(\overset{s}{\Sigma}X)^2}{s} = \underline{\hspace{4cm}} - \underline{\hspace{4cm}} =$$

$$SS_{TOTAL} = \overset{a\,s}{\Sigma\Sigma}X^2 - \frac{(\overset{a}{\Sigma}\overset{s}{\Sigma}X)^2}{as} = \underline{\hspace{4cm}} - \underline{\hspace{4cm}} =$$

MEAN SQ = S^2

$$S_A{}^2 = \frac{SS \text{ between}}{a - 1} = \underline{\hspace{5cm}} =$$

$$S_{S(A)}{}^2 = \frac{SS \text{ within}}{as - a} = \underline{\hspace{5cm}} =$$

H_o: $\sigma_\mu{}^2 = 0$

H_1: $\sigma_\mu{}^2 > 0$

$\alpha = .05$

Obtained F $= \dfrac{S_A{}^2}{S_{S(A)}{}^2} = \underline{\hspace{3cm}} =$

See "F" Table for Critical F Value, F $= \underline{\hspace{2cm}}$

$$df = \frac{}{(a - 1)} , \frac{}{(as - a)}$$

Conclusion: (If obtained value is *more* than critical value, reject H_o)

Decision: $\underline{\hspace{10cm}}$

FORM
Newman-Keuls Multiple Comparison Procedure
Following ANOVA

Tests: After significant F test, use Newman-Keuls to test any significant differences between means.

Necessary Terms: α = ._____ df = _____ n = _____ (one group)

Formula: $\qquad s_{\overline{m}} = \sqrt{\dfrac{s^2_{s}(D)}{n}}$ and $\qquad \overline{A}_1 - \overline{A}_2 = q\,(s_m)$

When $S^2_{S(D)}$ = within variance found in MS column of F table. $S^2_{S(D)}$ is the denominator in an F ratio.

$\overline{A}$ = mean of group A.

q = tabled value in Table J in the Appendix, the Studentized Range Statistic. First find df in left column, then decide .95 or .99 significance level, then the number of steps between ordered means. Multiply q times $S_{\overline{M}}$ and then subtract the two means. When difference between two means is more than q times $S_{\overline{M}}$ product, difference is significant.

Compute data:

Results:

FORM **TWO-WAY ANOVA** **Musical Example:**
(same as One-Way ANOVA)

Data Table

	A_1 (s = 13)	A_2 (s = 13)	A_3 (s = 13)	
B_1 (n = 39)	16 12 8 10 12 14 14 14 15 8 10 11 12 $\bar{X}=12$ $\Sigma A_1 B_1$ 156	16 14 12 10 13 14 12 13 14 10 10 12 13 $\bar{X}=12.54$ $\Sigma A_2 B_1$ 163	14 12 10 9 8 10 12 11 13 8 11 7 6 $\bar{X}=10.08$ $\Sigma A_3 B_1$ 131	B_1 $\Sigma X = 450$ $\Sigma X^2 = 5,422$ $(\Sigma X)^2 = 202,500$ $\bar{B}_1 = 11.54$
B_2 (n = 39)	7 6 8 12 7 6 5 8 7 11 10 9 10 $\bar{X}=8.15$ $\Sigma A_1 B_2$ 106	10 12 10 12 11 12 13 10 15 12 11 10 11 $\bar{X}=11.46$ $\Sigma A_2 B_2$ 149	5 9 10 5 6 4 9 11 7 8 9 10 9 $\bar{X}=7.85$ $\Sigma A_3 B_2$ 102	B_2 $\Sigma X = 357$ $\Sigma X^2 = 3,511$ $(\Sigma X)^2 = 127,449$ $\bar{B}_2 = 9.15$

Effective methods to improve articulation. 78 undergraduates in music are randomly chosen. 3 equal sized groups, 1/2 male, & 1/2 female, perform articulation exercise. All study over 10 week period and take posttest.

A_1 = teacher talks

A_2 = teacher model

A_3 = no contact control group

B_1 = male students

B_2 = female students

a = # of groups	3
b = # of sets	2
ab (groups x sets)	6
s = # of subjects	13
abs = TOTAL	78

(NECESSARY TERMS)

	A_1	A_2	A_3			
ΣX	262	312	233	→	$\overset{a\,b\,s}{\Sigma\Sigma\Sigma}X$	807
ΣX^2	2,868	3,816	2,249	→	$\overset{a\,b\,s}{\Sigma\Sigma\Sigma}X^2$ = 8,933	(5)
$(\Sigma X)^2$	68,644	97,344	54,289	→	$\overset{a\ \ b\,s}{\Sigma}(\Sigma\Sigma X)^2$ = 220,277	
A_a	10.08	12.00	8.96		$\dfrac{\overset{a\ \ b\,s}{\Sigma}(\Sigma\Sigma X)^2}{b\,s}$ = 8,472.19	(1)*

CHECK NECESSARY TERMS, is

(5) > (1) or (2) or (3) > (4) ? <u>Yes</u>

8,933 > <u>8,472.19</u> or <u>8,460.23</u> or <u>8,608.23</u>

> <u>8,349.35</u>

*(1) $\dfrac{\overset{a\ \ b\,s}{\Sigma}(\Sigma\Sigma X)^2}{b\,s} = \dfrac{(220,277)}{26}$

(2) $\dfrac{\overset{b\ \ a\,s}{\Sigma}(\Sigma\Sigma X)^2}{a\,s} = \dfrac{202,500 + 127,449}{39}$

(3) $\dfrac{\overset{a\,b\ \ s}{\Sigma\Sigma}(\Sigma X)^2}{s} = \dfrac{(156)^2 + (163)^2 \ldots + (102)^2}{13}$

(4) $\dfrac{\overset{a\,b\,s}{(\Sigma\Sigma\Sigma X)^2}}{a\,b\,s} = \dfrac{651,249}{78}$

$\dfrac{\overset{b\ \ a\,s}{\Sigma}(\Sigma\Sigma X)^2}{a\,s}$ = 8,460.23	(2)
$\dfrac{\overset{a\,b\ \ s}{\Sigma\Sigma}(\Sigma X)^2}{s}$ = 8,608.23	(3)
$\overset{a\,b\,s}{(\Sigma\Sigma\Sigma X)^2}$ = 651,249	
$\dfrac{\overset{a\,b\,s}{(\Sigma\Sigma\Sigma X)^2}}{a\,b\,s}$ = 8,349.35	(4)
$\bar{M}$ = 10.35	

BASIC PROCEDURES IN TWO-WAY ANOVA TABLE

Source	SS (Necessary Terms)	df	MS (σ^2)	F
A	(1) − (4)	(a − 1)	SS_A/df_A	$MS_A/MS_{S(AB)}$
B	(2) − (4)	(b − 1)	SS_B/df_B	$MS_B/MS_{S(AB)}$
AB	(3) − (1) − (2) + (4)	(a−1)(b−1)	SS_{AB}/df_{AB}	$MS_{AB}/MS_{S(AB)}$
S(AB)	(5) − (3)	(abs−ab)	$SS_{S(AB)}/df_{S(AB)}$	———
Total	(5) − (4)	(abs−1)	———	———

TWO-WAY ANOVA TABLE
Data from Musical Example

Source	SS	df	MS	F
A	122.84	2	61.42	13.62
B	110.88	1	110.88	24.59
AB	25.16	2	12.58	2.79
S(AB)	324.77	72	4.51	———
Total	583.65	77	———	———

STATISTICAL DECISION
Based on Data From Above

Source	df	Critical "F" ($\alpha = .05$) (Table H in Appendix)	Obtained "F"	Decision
A	2,72	3.15	13.62	Significant differences, reject H_o
B	1,72	4.00	24.59	Significant difference, reject H_o
AB	2,72	3.15	2.79	*No* significant interaction, do *not* reject H_o

Compute This Musical Example

TWO-WAY ANALYSIS OF VARIANCE DATA TABLE

	A_1 (s = 5)	A_2 (s = 5)	A_3 (s = 5)	Sum of B's	
B_1	3 2 2 $\overline{X}$ = 1 $\Sigma A_1 B_1$ = 1	4 4 3 $\overline{X}$ = 3 $\Sigma A_2 B_1$ = 3	5 5 4 $\overline{X}$ = 4 $\Sigma A_3 B_1$ = 4	B_1 n = 15 ΣX = ΣX^2 = $(\Sigma X)^2$ = $\overline{B_1}$ =	
B_2	3 3 2 $\overline{X}$ = 2 $\Sigma A_1 B_2$ = 2	3 2 2 $\overline{X}$ = 1 $\Sigma A_2 B_2$ = 1	2 2 2 $\overline{X}$ = 1 $\Sigma A_3 B_2$ = 1	B_2 n = 15 ΣX = ΣX^2 = $(\Sigma X)^2$ = $\overline{B_2}$ =	
Sum A's ΣX			$\longrightarrow$	a b s $\Sigma\Sigma\Sigma$ X	(Necessary Terms)
ΣX^2			$\longrightarrow$	a b s $\Sigma\Sigma\Sigma$ X^2	(5)
$(\Sigma X)^2$			$\longrightarrow$	a b s Σ $(\Sigma\Sigma X)^2$	
$\overline{A}_a$				a b s Σ $(\Sigma\Sigma X)^2$ b s	(1)
				b a s Σ $(\Sigma\Sigma X)^2$ a s	(2)
				a b s $\Sigma\Sigma$ $(\Sigma X)^2$ s	(3)
				a b s $(\Sigma\Sigma\Sigma X)^2$	
				a b s $(\Sigma\Sigma\Sigma X)^2$ a b s	(4)
				$\overline{M}$	

Study: Distraction during practice time. 30 high school band students (15 advanced and 15 beginning). S's record number of distractions in 1/2 hour of practice time. Data collected after one semester of the treatments.

A_1 = sensitized by teacher

A_2 = use tape recorder

A_3 = no contact control

B_1

Beginning band

B_2

Advanced band

a = # of groups _____

b = # of sets _____

s = # of subjects _____

ab = (a) $\times$ (b) _____

abs = TOTAL _____

Check Necessary Terms, is:

(5) > (1) or (2) or (3) > (4) ?

Musical Example (Continued)
TWO-WAY ANALYSIS OF VARIANCE
BASIC PROCEDURES IN TWO-WAY ANOVA TABLE

Source	SS (Necessary Terms)	df	MS (σ^2)	F
A	(1) − (4)	$(a - 1)$	SS_A / df_A	$MS_A / MS_{S(AB)}$
B	(2) − (4)	$(b - 1)$	SS_B / df_B	$MS_B / MS_{S(AB)}$
AB	(3) − (1) − (2) + (4)	$(a-1)(b-1)$	SS_{AB} / df_{AB}	$MS_{AB} / MS_{S(AB)}$
S(AB)	(5) − (3)	$(abs-ab)$	$SS_{S(AB)} / df_{S(AB)}$	———
Total	(5) − (4)	$(abs-1)$	———	———

TWO-WAY ANOVA TABLE
(Fill-in Data)

Source	SS	df	MS	F
A				
B				
AB				
S(AB)				
Total				

STATISTICAL DECISION
(Based on Data Above)

Source	df	Critical "F" ($\alpha = .05$) (Table H in Appendix)	Obtained "F" (data above)	Decision, if obtained value is greater, then reject H_o
A				
B				
AB				GRAPH SIGNIFICANT INTERACTION

Obtained F: A = 4.74   B = 28   AB = 17.28
All are significant at .05 level.   ∴ Reject H_o

TWO-WAY ANALYSIS OF VARIANCE DATA TABLE (2 $\times$ 3)

	A_1 (s =)	A_2 (s =)	A_3 (s =)	Sum of B's	
B_1	$\overline{X}$ = $\Sigma A_1 B_1$	$\overline{X}$ = $\Sigma A_2 B_1$	$\overline{X}$ = $\Sigma A_3 B_1$	B_1 n = ΣX = ΣX^2 = $(\Sigma X)^2$ = $\overline{B}_1$ =	
B_2	$\overline{X}$ = $\Sigma A_1 B_2$	$\overline{X}$ = $\Sigma A_2 B_2$	$\overline{X}$ = $\Sigma A_3 B_2$	B_2 n = ΣX = ΣX^2 = $(\Sigma X)^2$ = $\overline{B}_2$ =	
Sum A's $\Sigma\ X$				a b s $\Sigma\Sigma\Sigma X$	**(Necessary Terms)**
$\Sigma\ X^2$				a b s $\Sigma\Sigma\Sigma X^2$	(5)
$(\Sigma X)^2$				a b s $\Sigma\ (\Sigma\Sigma X)^2$	
$\overline{A}_a$				a b s $\Sigma\ \dfrac{(\Sigma\Sigma X)^2}{b\ s}$	(1)

Study: _____

_____

_____

_____

_____

b a s $\Sigma\ \dfrac{(\Sigma\Sigma X)^2}{a\ s}$	(2)
a b s $\Sigma\Sigma\ \dfrac{(\Sigma X)^2}{s}$	(3)
a b s $(\Sigma\Sigma\Sigma X)^2$	
a b s $\dfrac{(\Sigma\Sigma\Sigma X)^2}{a\ b\ s}$	(4)
$\overline{M}$	

A_1 = B_1 =

A_2 =

A_3 = B_2 =

a = _____   ab = _____

b = _____   abs = _____

s = _____

Check NECESSARY TERMS, is:

(5) > (1) or (2) or (3) > (4) ?

FORM
Musical Example (Continued)
TWO-WAY ANALYSIS OF VARIANCE
BASIC PROCEDURES IN TWO-WAY ANOVA TABLE

Source	SS (Necessary Terms)	df	MS (σ^2)	F
A	$(1) - (4)$	$(a - 1)$	SS_A/df_A	$MS_A/MS_{S(AB)}$
B	$(2) - (4)$	$(b - 1)$	SS_B/df_B	$MS_B/MS_{S(AB)}$
AB	$(3) - (1) - (2) + (4)$	$(a-1)(b-1)$	SS_{AB}/df_{AB}	$MS_{AB}/MS_{S(AB)}$
S(AB)	$(5) - (3)$	$(abs-ab)$	$SS_{S(AB)}/df_{S(AB)}$	———
Total	$(5) - (4)$	$(abs-1)$	———	———

TWO-WAY ANOVA TABLE
(Fill-in Data)

Source	SS	df	MS	F
A				
B				
AB				
S(AB)				
Total				

STATISTICAL DECISION
(Based on Data Above)

Source	df	Critical "F" ($\alpha = .05$) (Table H in Appendix)	Obtained "F" (data above)	Decision, if obtained value is greater, then reject H_o
A				
B				
AB				GRAPH SIGNIFICANT INTERACTION

Obtained F: A = 5.10   B = 31.58   AB = 18.58
All are significant at .05 level.   ∴ Reject H_o

INTERACTION IN MULTIFACTOR ANALYSIS

Interaction means that the effect of one variable (A) is not similar or parallel across all levels of the other variable (B). This AB interaction may take the two forms shown below.

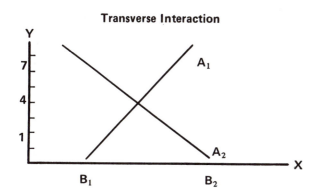

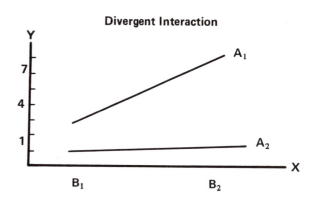

1. Transverse Interaction

As pictured above, if we consider the effect of A_1 alone, it increases from 1 to 7 as we go from B_1 to B_2. Conversely, the effect of A_2 decreases from 7 to 1 as we go from B_1 to B_2. Moreover, the overall effect (across all B levels) of A_1 is 4 and so is the overall effect for A_2. Thus the overall A means are not different from each other, or the effect of A is said to be insignificant. Similarly the overall effect of B_1 and B_2 is also 4, so the effect of factor B is also shown to be apparently nonsignificant. Clearly A_1 is different from A_2 at *both* B levels, but because of the crossover effect the overall algebraic values of all A's are equal. This transverse relationship obviously militates against any meaningful significance of (or even test of) the main effect of A or B alone. In most cases of a transverse interaction the main effects will not be significant. However, if the AB interaction is significant, then the two factors *must* have significant effects. You cannot have a significant interaction between two insignificant effects. Of course, the effects are limited to specific levels of A and B and no general statements can be made.

2. Divergent Interaction

The second graph indicates another form of nonparallel or interaction relationship between factors A and B. In this case the overall value of A_1 is about 5 and A_2 is about 1.5. Therefore the differences between the A means may lead to a significant main effect of factor A. Similarly B_1 overall value is 2 and B_2 is about 4.5. Again these differences may lead to a significant B effect. Thus in a divergent type of AB interaction, either variable A or B or both may be significant and you may conclude that *in general* certain A (or B) levels are different from other levels of A. But if the AB interaction is also significant, then you must qualify the conclusions concerning variable A (or B) because this effect, while acting in the same direction, acts with greater magnitude at certain levels of the other factor. (Lines A and B are often called X and Y).

REVIEW OF INTERACTION PRINCIPLES

1. XY interaction may occur only so long as each unit of X appears under each unit of Y. (Obviously there can never be an XY interaction if one of the factors is "nested" within the other; e.g., no AS interaction in an S(A) design because different S's are nested within different A groups.)

2. XY interaction may be *measured* (and correctly identified) so long as there is at least one score in each XY cell and this score is not "confounded" with another effect. (This becomes important later when considering the Latin Square designs.)

3. XY interaction may be *evaluated* only so long as there are at least 2 independent observations made at each XY cell. (No F ratio is possible because no $S^2_{s(xy)}$ is obtained for testing S^2_{xy}.)

S_{abs} (A_aB_b) design

	A_2	. . . .	Aa
B_1	s_1 $\vdots$ s_s		
B_b			

AB occurs

AB measured $\qquad S^2_{AB}$

AB evaluated $\qquad \dfrac{S^2_{AB}}{S^2_{S(AB)}}$

S_{ab} (A_aB_b) design: 1 S/cell

	A_1	. . . .	Aa
B_1	S_1		
.	S_2		
.	.		
.	.		
.	.		
B_b	S_s		

AB occurs

AB measured $\qquad S^2_{AB}$

AB *not* evaluated. Must have at least 2 scores in each cell to get
$$S^2_{S(AB)}$$

In the following graphs, determine where significant interaction effects might occur:

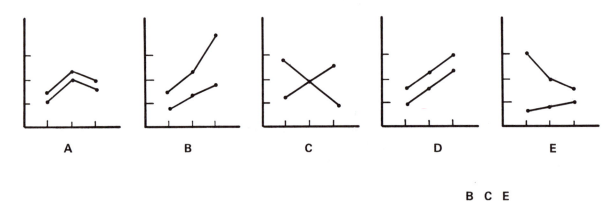

| A | B | C | D | E |

B C E

Coefficient of Correlation

The coefficient of correlation (r) is a single value (number) used to represent the relationship between two sets of data representing continuous variables which have been collected for the same individual or which can be paired in some manner. In other words, it represents the extent to which changes in one variable are accompanied by equal changes in another; or the degree to which the data, when plotted, fall into a straight line.

110

A Positive Linear Relationship (r = 1.00)

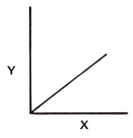

A Negative Linear Relationship (r = −1.00)

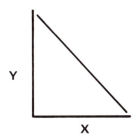

No Relationship (r = 0.00)

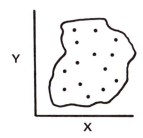

The most common form of correlation coefficient is the Pearson "Product-Moment" correlation. This correlation coefficient assumes three things about the data:

1. Both variables are continuous.
2. An interval or ratio level of measurement.
3. A linear relationship exists between the two variables.

It should be remembered that correlation is a necessary but not a sufficient condition for causation. That is, two variables may be related but this does not necessarily mean that changes in one variable cause change in the other. For example, the production of pig iron in the U.S. may be highly correlated with the birth rate in China, but this does not mean that producing pig iron causes more babies to be born.

The Pearson "Product-Moment" correlation is defined as the average of the product of the Z scores for two groups and is computed from the following "raw score" formula:

$$r_{xy} = \frac{N\Sigma XY - (\Sigma X)(\Sigma Y)}{\sqrt{[N\Sigma X^2 - (\Sigma X)^2][N\Sigma Y^2 - (\Sigma Y)^2]}}$$

Thus by knowing the following list of necessary terms, one can compute the correlation coefficient:

$$\Sigma X \quad \Sigma Y \quad \Sigma X^2 \quad \Sigma Y^2 \quad \Sigma XY \quad \text{and} \quad N$$

PROBLEMS FOR
REVIEW OF CORRELATION COEFFICIENT

1. The following scores on two auditory tests were earned by 10 prospective band students. How well do the scores correlate? Would they make good band members?

Student	Test #1	Test #2
1	7	9
2	7	9
3	7	9
4	8	9
5	9	10
6	6	9
7	7	9
8	7	9
9	8	9
10	9	10

Answer: 1. $\Sigma X = 75$ N = 10
$\Sigma Y = 92$ r = .82
$\Sigma X^2 = 571$ Since both tests correlate at .82,
$\Sigma Y^2 = 848$ this high agreement would indicate
$\Sigma XY = 693$ these 10 students would probably make good band members.

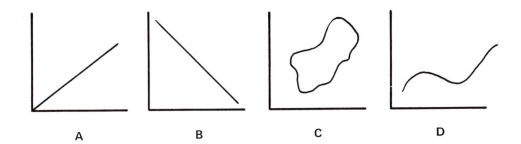

2. Which figure represents a nonlinear relationship?

3. Which figure represents a negative linear relationship?

4. Which figure represents a positively skewed curve?

5. Which figure represents a zero correlation?

6. Which figure represents a positive linear relationship?

7. Suppose you had scores from a reading test and an arithmetic test for a group of 10 students. Let X represent the reading test scores and Y represent the arithmetic scores. Given the following information compute the Pearson Product-Moment correlation coefficient between the reading test and the arithmetic test.

$$\Sigma X = 60$$
$$\Sigma Y = 50$$
$$\Sigma XY = 334$$
$$\Sigma X^2 = 420$$
$$\Sigma Y^2 = 290$$

Answers:

2.	D	5.	C
3.	B	6.	A
4.	None	7.	$r = .69$

Spearman Rank Correlation Coefficient
(Siegel, 1956)

Tests: Measures the association of two variables done by one individual. . . . Two variables are ranked separately and the ranks are correlated. . . . A nonparametric alternative to the Pearson "Product Moment" correlation. . . . Assumes that both variables are measured in at least an ordinal scale.

Hypotheses: None, this is *not* a test of hypothesis but rather a test of correlation between two variables. Spearman Rank Correlation Coefficient measures the *degree* of association between two sets of scores.

Level of Significance: This correlation measures the *extent* to which one variable is associated with another variable. . . *not* the probability or existence of an association to a population.

Rationale in Example: Take N number of students and rank them according to two variables, such as, college entrance test and GPA. Suzie ranks 5th in her class on the entrance test and 2nd in her class in GPA. Sammy ranks 8th in his class on the college entrance test and 4th in his class in GPA. The difference (d) in Suzie's ranks is 3 while Sammy's rank difference is 4. There is less difference in Suzie's rank d than Sammy's. If there were perfect correlation, each rank difference would be 0 (zero). The magnitude or degree of difference in association of two variables is what this test measures.

Procedure:

1. Rank observations on X variable from 1 to N. Rank observations on Y variable from 1 to N.
2. Subtract subject's Y rank from his X rank. Square this value to determine each subject's d^2 value.
3. Sum the d^2 for all subjects = Σd^2.
4. If number of ties exceed 25%, use tie formula on Form.
5. When N is from 4 to 30, use r formula and find critical value on Spearman Table at .05 or .01 level.
6. If $N \geq 10$, t formula may be utilized and its corresponding t Table for the critical value.
7. Decision states the degree of correlation between the two variables. No causality is expressed in the association of the two variables. That is, there may be high correlation (generally .70 or above) but one variable does not cause the other.

Musical Example*

Study: *Relation of Amount of Practice to Performance on a Qualifying Jury.* _____

_____

X   no. years studied musical instrument

Y   evaluation of a qualifying jury

When ties exceed 25% use following formula where

T = number of tied observations at a given rank

$$\Sigma\ x^2\ =\ \frac{N^3-N}{12}\ -\ \Sigma\ T_x$$

$$\Sigma\ y^2\ =\ \frac{N^3-N}{12}\ -\ \Sigma\ T_y$$

$$r\ =\ \frac{\Sigma\ x^2\ +\ \Sigma\ y^2\ -\ \Sigma\ d^2}{2\sqrt{\Sigma\ x^2\ \Sigma\ y^2}}$$

(optional)

$\underline{t}$ test (if N $\geq$ 10)

$$t\ =\ r\sqrt{\frac{N-2}{1-r^2}}$$

$$\overline{r\ =\ .943}$$

*(fabricated data)

Spearman Rank Correlation Coefficient

S No.	X	Rank X	Y	Rank Y	d^2
1	5	5	88	5	0
2	4	4	85	4	0
3	6	6	92	6	0
4	2	2	70	3	1
5	3	3	65	2	1
6	1	1	60	1	0
7					
8					
9					
10					
11					
12					
13					
14					
15					
16					
17					
18					
19					
20					

N = $\Sigma\ d^2$ =

$$r\ =\ 1\ -\ \frac{6\ \Sigma d^2}{N^3-N}$$

FORM

Spearman Rank Correlation Coefficient

Study: _____

_____

_____

_____

X _____

Y _____

When ties exceed 25% use
following formula where
T = number of tied
     observations at a
     given rank

$$\Sigma\ x^2 = \frac{N^3 - N}{12} - \Sigma\ T_x$$

$$\Sigma\ y^2 = \frac{N^3 - N}{12} - \Sigma\ T_y$$

$$r = \frac{\Sigma\ x^2 + \Sigma\ y^2 - \Sigma\ d^2}{2\sqrt{\Sigma\ x^2\ \Sigma\ y^2}}$$

S No.	X	Rank X	Y	Rank Y	d^2
1					
2					
3					
4					
5					
6					
7					
8					
9					
10					
11					
12					
13					
14					
15					
16					
17					
18					
19					
20					

N = $\Sigma\ d^2$ =

(Optional t test)
may use if N $\geq$ 10

$$t = r\sqrt{\frac{N - 2}{1 - r^2}}$$

$$r = 1 - \frac{6\ \Sigma d^2}{N^3 - N}$$

Appendix

GLOSSARY OF STATISTICAL SYMBOLS

α Alpha, the significance level (α) is the probability that a statistical test will yield a value under which the null hypothesis will be rejected when in fact it is true.

β Beta, the probability that a statistical test will yield a value under which the null hypothesis will be accepted when in fact it is false.

d   difference, usually between one score and another.

=   equals, as 5 = 5.

≠   unequal, such as, 5 ≠ 6.

±   either plus or minus direction possible; used in Confidence Intervals to indicate a spread or range above and below a numerical value.

>   greater than sign, i.e., 9 > 4.

<   less than sign, i.e., 10 < 20.

≥   equal to or greater than sign. A ≥ a.

≤   equal to or less than sign. b ≤ B.

df   degrees of freedom, the number of times a random choice is allowed to vary before it is fixed with a given sample.

χ^2 Chi Square, the most frequently used statistic in nonparametrics.

F   the F statistic, used in the parametric statistics analysis of variance test (ANOVA).

ANOVA analysis of variance parametric, statistical design.

H   Kruskal-Wallis statistic; nonparametric one way analysis of variance.

H_o null hypothesis, an *a priori* statement of no differences.

H_1 alternate hypothesis (sometimes given as H_a); two-tailed alternative allows that differences exist, while a one-tailed alternative hypothesizes a direction for any differences.

k   column; a vertical grouping in a data table, as opposed to a row which is horizontal across a data table.

μ Mu, Greek letter for population mean.

N   number in all groups, a total number of subjects or scores.

n   number in a single group, as n_1 = number in group one, n_2 = number in group two, etc.

p   probability, the likelihood an event will occur by chance.

r   row, horizontal grouping in a data table.

R(r)   Correlation, the relation or association of two variables, Statistic used in the Pearson Product-Moment correlation and Spearman Rank correlation.

Σ sum, $\Sigma(4 + 3) = 7$ (Greek for "Sigma").

S.D.   standard deviation.

s   standard deviation of a sample, the square root of the sample variance.

s^2 sample variance, $s^2 = \dfrac{\Sigma(X - \overline{X})^2}{N - 1}$

σ	standard deviation of a population.
σ^2	variance of a population.
X^2	score X squared, for example, if $X = 12$, $X^2 = (12)^2 = 144$.
$\sqrt{X}$	square root of X, if $X = 121$, $\sqrt{121} = 11$.
t	t statistic, parametric test which compares the means of two groups.
T	value of the Wilcoxon Matched-Pairs Signed Ranks statistic, nonparametric test comparing two dependent groups.
U	statistic of the Mann-Whitney U test, nonparametric test for two independent groups.
X	a sample score from group X.
$\overline{X}$	mean or average score for group X, called "bar" X.
Y	a sample score from group Y.
Z	a standard score, a value that indicates the amount by which a raw score deviates from the mean ($\overline{X}$) in standard deviation units. Z scores are a closed system and any Z scores from different distributions of scores are directly comparable.

BASIC MATHEMATICAL PROCEDURES
Algebra

1. Order of operation:
   A. Do all multiplication and division, then addition and subtraction.

   Example: $3 + 4 \times 5 - 7 = 3 + 20 - 7 = 16$

   B. If there are grouping signs, such as, parenthesis or brackets, then work within the grouping signs first.

   Example: $(3 + 4) \times 5 - 7 = 7 \times 5 - 7 = 28$

2. Fractions:
   A. Multiplication.

   Example: $3/4 \times 5/7 = 15/28$

   B. Division.

   Example: $3/4 \div 5/7 = 3/4 \times 7/5 = 21/20$

   (Work fractions to lowest common denominator and leave as a fraction and not a mixed number.)

   C. Addition and subtraction.

   Examples: $3/4 + 7/4 = 10/4 = 5/2$

   $3/4 + 7/8 = 6/8 + 7/8 = 15/8$

   $4/5 - 2/3 = 12/15 - 10/15 = 2/15$

3. Operations with signed numbers:
   A. Addition and subtraction.

   Examples: $(-7) + (-3) = -10$

   $-7 - 3 = -10$

   $(-7) - (+3) = -10$

   $-4 + 3 - 10 = -11$

   (1) $(-) + (-) = -$

   (2) $(+) + (+) = +$

B. Multiplication and division.

Examples: $(-7) \times (-3) = +21$

$(-4)(+5) = -20$

(1) Same signs $= +$

(2) Opposite signs $= -$

4. Radicals:

A. Theorem of square roots.

Examples: $\sqrt[n]{a}$ $\sqrt[1]{4} = 2$ $\sqrt[3]{8} = 2$ (check, $2^3 = 8$)

B. Theorem for multiplying radicals.

Examples: $\sqrt{a}$ $\sqrt{b} = \sqrt{ab}$ $\sqrt{7}\sqrt{6} = \sqrt{42}$

C. Theorem for dividing radicals.

Examples: $\dfrac{\sqrt{a}}{\sqrt{b}} = \sqrt{\dfrac{a}{b}}$ $\dfrac{\sqrt{6}}{\sqrt{2}} = \sqrt{\dfrac{6}{2}} = \sqrt{3}$

5. Exponents:

A. Theorem for squares.

Example: $a^n = (a)(a)(a) \dots (a_n)$ $n = n$ times

$a^4 = (a)(a)(a)(a)$

B. Theorem on exponent of zero.

Example: $a = 1$ $a \neq 0$ $1^a = 1$ $1^a \neq 0$

$(10)^\circ = 1$ $(4/5)^0 = 1$

C. Theorem for multiplying exponents.

Example: $a^m a^n = a^{m+n}$

$3^4 3^5 = 3^{4+5} = 3^9$

D. Theorem for dividing exponents.

Example: $\dfrac{a^m}{a^n}$ a^{m-n}

$\dfrac{3^4}{3^3} = 3^{4-3} = 3^1 = 3$

E. Definition of negative exponent.

Example: $a^{-n} = \dfrac{1}{a^n}$ $2^{-3} = \dfrac{1}{2^3} = \dfrac{1}{8}$

F. Definition of fractional exponents.

Example: $a^{1/n} = \sqrt[n]{a}$ $4^{1/2} = \sqrt[2]{4}$

6. Equation procedures:

A. Squaring parenthesis.

Example: $(a + b)^2 = a^2 + 2ab + b^2$

B. Signs in double groupings.

Example: $\Sigma[X_1 - (\overline{X} + C)]^2 = \Sigma[X_1 - \overline{X} - C]^2$

7. Extraction of Square Roots

```
                2 7 1. 7 8
        2|√73869.0320
                4
       47|   338
             329
      541|     969
              541
     5427|    42803
             37989
    54348|     481420
             434784
              46636
```

A check on accuracy

```
                271.79
                271.79
               2446.11
              19025.3
              27179
             190253
              54358
            73869.8041
```

Step 1: Mark off numbers by pairs to both right and left of decimal point (73869.0320).

Step 2: Determine the square root of the first unit (7), record this number (2), and record the square of this number (4).

Step 3: Subtract as in long division (7 − 4 = 3) and bring down the next pair of numbers (38).

Step 4: Double the quotient obtained thus far (2), add a tenative 0 to this value, and record this number (40) to the left of the remainder (338).

Step 5: Determine how many times this value (40) will go into the remainder (338) and record this value (7) in the answer. Add this value (7) to the divisor (40 + 7 = 47). Multiply as in long division (7 × 47 = 329) and record this value.

Step 6: Repeat steps 3, 4, and 5 until the problem is completed.

Step 7: Check your accuracy by squaring the answer (271.79 × 271.79 = 73869.8041).

USE OF A BURROUGHS CALCULATOR
FOR ANOVA

In the computation of large numbers and/or samples, a calculator is a convenient tool to facilitate paper work. The Burroughs Calculator is frequently found in libraries and areas of experimental research. Most machines have a booklet explaining the basic operations. Read this first.

The following steps outline a procedure to ease computation in the ANOVA (parametric analysis of variance).

Method of summing scores and their squares simultaneously.

1. Calculator on.
2. Clear all numbers from window and memory banks.
3. Push up two buttons in upper-left to turn on memory banks.
4. Enter number, go down column one with steps 4, 5, and 6.
5. Depress ×(times) key and one bank lights up.
6. Press $\pm$ (add-equals) key and other bank lights up.
7. Continue steps 4, 5, and 6 until all numbers in one column are entered.
8. Push ◇ key on II = ΣX. Write It Down.
9. Push ◇ key on I = ΣX^2. Write It Down.
10. Clear memory banks I and II.
11. Procedure to enter each number from column two following steps 4-10 above.
12. Do steps 4-10 for each column until complete.

13. To obtain total sum of scores, $\Sigma\Sigma X$, add all the sums shown on memory bank II (step 8 above).

14. To find the total sum of squares, $\Sigma\Sigma X^2$, add all the sums shown previously on memory bank I (step 9 above).

15. To determine F value, procedures on the calculator following the ANOVA *Form* are easier than on paper. Follow *Form* and perform all basic division and subtraction with the calculator.

READING STATISTICAL TABLES

A. *Z* Normal Distribution: Directions on table. Find probability if $Z = 2.34$ ... one-tailed $p = .0096$. To determine the two-tailed probability, double the tabled p value. ... When $Z = 1.96$, what is two-tailed p? (Answers at bottom.)

B. Chi Square: First determine df (vertical axis) and α level (horizontal axis). Then find Chi Square critical value where these two axes cross. ... For example, if df = 15 and $\alpha = .05$, what is critical Chi Square?

C. Wilcoxon Matched-Pairs Signed-Ranks: Find N value (left column) and significance level (top rows). Critical value of "T" is where the appropriate column and row cross. ... Example, if $N = 18$ and two-tailed $\alpha = .01$, what is the critical "T" value?

D. Mann-Whitney U: When $n_2 < 9$, specify size of n_2 for correct table, then size of n_1 and U will give critical p. Example: if $n_2 = 6$, $n_1 = 4$ and $U = 11$, what is p? ... When $n_2 > 8$, specify exact α (level and tails), then n_1 and n_2 give critical U. If $\alpha = .05$, two-tailed and $n_1 = 10$, and $n_2 = 15$, U will equal?

E. Friedman Two-Way ANOVA by Ranks: Specify k, N and obtained χ^2 values. The p value is right adjacent to the χ^2 value. For example, if $k = 3$, $N = 8$ and $\chi^2 = 6.25$, what is p?

F. Kruskal-Wallis One-Way ANOVA by Ranks: Determine sample sizes (n_1, n_2, n_3) and obtained H Value. p is found right adjacent to the H value. ... Example: $n_1 = 5$, $n_2 = 3$, $n_3 = 1$, $H = 4.890$, what is the nearest probability?

G. *t* Table: When df and α are known, critical t is found. For example: if df = 12 and two-tailed $\alpha = .01$, the critical $t = 3.055$. ... When df = 19, two-tailed $\alpha = .05$, what is p?

H. *F* Distribution: Specify v_1 (df for numerator of F ratio) and v_2 (df for denominator in F ratio). Critical F value is found from these two points of reference. ... For example: When $v_1 = 10$, $v_2 = 17$, critical F = 2.45. If $v_1 = 5$, $v_2 = 27$, what is the critical F?

I. Spearman Rank Correlation Coefficient: Size of N gives the corresponding critical value at the right. For example: If N = 12, what are the critical values?

A = .0500	D = .457 and 39	G = 2.093
B = 25.00	E = .047	H = 2.57
C = 28	F = .052	I = (.05) .506
		(.01) .712

List of Tables

APPENDIX

Table A. Table of Probabilities Associated with Values as Extreme as Observed Values of z in the Normal Distribution

The body of the table gives one-tailed probabilities under H_0 of z. The left-hand marginal column gives various values of z to one decimal place. The top row gives various values to the second decimal place. Thus, for example, the one-tailed p of $z \geq .11$ or $z \leq -.11$ is $p = .4562$.

z	.00	.01	.02	.03	.04	.05	.06	.07	.08	.09
.0	.5000	.4960	.4920	.4880	.4840	.4801	.4761	.4721	.4681	.4641
.1	.4602	.4562	.4522	.4483	.4443	.4404	.4364	.4325	.4286	.4247
.2	.4207	.4168	.4129	.4090	.4052	.4013	.3974	.3936	.3897	.3859
.3	.3821	.3783	.3745	.3707	.3669	.3632	.3594	.3557	.3520	.3483
.4	.3446	.3409	.3372	.3336	.3300	.3264	.3228	.3192	.3156	.3121
.5	.3085	.3050	.3015	.2981	.2946	.2912	.2877	.2843	.2810	.2776
.6	.2743	.2709	.2676	.2643	.2611	.2578	.2546	.2514	.2483	.2451
.7	.2420	.2389	.2358	.2327	.2296	.2266	.2236	.2206	.2177	.2148
.8	.2119	.2090	.2061	.2033	.2005	.1977	.1949	.1922	.1894	.1867
.9	.1841	.1814	.1788	.1762	.1736	.1711	.1685	.1660	.1635	.1611
1.0	.1587	.1562	.1539	.1515	.1492	.1469	.1446	.1423	.1401	.1379
1.1	.1357	.1335	.1314	.1292	.1271	.1251	.1230	.1210	.1190	.1170
1.2	.1151	.1131	.1112	.1093	.1075	.1056	.1038	.1020	.1003	.0985
1.3	.0968	.0951	.0934	.0918	.0901	.0885	.0869	.0853	.0838	.0823
1.4	.0808	.0793	.0778	.0764	.0749	.0735	.0721	.0708	.0694	.0681
1.5	.0668	.0655	.0643	.0630	.0618	.0606	.0594	.0582	.0571	.0559
1.6	.0548	.0537	.0526	.0516	.0505	.0495	.0485	.0475	.0465	.0455
1.7	.0446	.0436	.0427	.0418	.0409	.0401	.0392	.0384	.0375	.0367
1.8	.0359	.0351	.0344	.0336	.0329	.0322	.0314	.0307	.0301	.0294
1.9	.0287	.0281	.0274	.0268	.0262	.0256	.0250	.0244	.0239	.0233
2.0	.0228	.0222	.0217	.0212	.0207	.0202	.0197	.0192	.0188	.0183
2.1	.0179	.0174	.0170	.0166	.0162	.0158	.0154	.0150	.0146	.0143
2.2	.0139	.0136	.0132	.0129	.0125	.0122	.0119	.0116	.0113	.0110
2.3	.0107	.0104	.0102	.0099	.0096	.0094	.0091	.0089	.0087	.0084
2.4	.0082	.0080	.0078	.0075	.0073	.0071	.0069	.0068	.0066	.0064
2.5	.0062	.0060	.0059	.0057	.0055	.0054	.0052	.0051	.0049	.0048
2.6	.0047	.0045	.0044	.0043	.0041	.0040	.0039	.0038	.0037	.0036
2.7	.0035	.0034	.0033	.0032	.0031	.0030	.0029	.0028	.0027	.0026
2.8	.0026	.0025	.0024	.0023	.0023	.0022	.0021	.0021	.0020	.0019
2.9	.0019	.0018	.0018	.0017	.0016	.0016	.0015	.0015	.0014	.0014
3.0	.0013	.0013	.0013	.0012	.0012	.0011	.0011	.0011	.0010	.0010
3.1	.0010	.0009	.0009	.0009	.0008	.0008	.0008	.0008	.0007	.0007
3.2	.0007									
3.3	.0005									
3.4	.0003									
3.5	.00023									
3.6	.00016									
3.7	.00011									
3.8	.00007									
3.9	.00005									
4.0	.00003									

APPENDIX

Table B. Table of Critical Values of Chi Square

df	.99	.98	.95	.90	.80	.70	.50	.30	.20	.10	.05	.02	.01	.001
1	.00016	.00063	.0039	.016	.064	.15	.46	1.07	1.64	2.71	3.84	5.41	6.64	10.83
2	.02	.04	.10	.21	.45	.71	1.39	2.41	3.22	4.60	5.99	7.82	9.21	13.82
3	.12	.18	.35	.58	1.00	1.42	2.37	3.66	4.64	6.25	7.82	9.84	11.34	16.27
4	.30	.43	.71	1.06	1.65	2.20	3.36	4.88	5.99	7.78	9.49	11.67	13.28	18.46
5	.55	.75	1.14	1.61	2.34	3.00	4.35	6.06	7.29	9.24	11.07	13.39	15.09	20.52
6	.87	1.13	1.64	2.20	3.07	3.83	5.35	7.23	8.56	10.64	12.59	15.03	16.81	22.46
7	1.24	1.56	2.17	2.83	3.82	4.67	6.35	8.38	9.80	12.02	14.07	16.62	18.48	24.32
8	1.65	2.03	2.73	3.49	4.59	5.53	7.34	9.52	11.03	13.36	15.51	18.17	20.09	26.12
9	2.09	2.53	3.32	4.17	5.38	6.39	8.34	10.66	12.24	14.68	16.92	19.68	21.67	27.88
10	2.56	3.06	3.94	4.86	6.18	7.27	9.34	11.78	13.44	15.99	18.31	21.16	23.21	29.59
11	3.05	3.61	4.58	5.58	6.99	8.15	10.34	12.90	14.63	17.28	19.68	22.62	24.72	31.26
12	3.57	4.18	5.23	6.30	7.81	9.03	11.34	14.01	15.81	18.55	21.03	24.05	26.22	32.91
13	4.11	4.76	5.89	7.04	8.63	9.93	12.34	15.12	16.98	19.81	22.36	25.47	27.69	34.53
14	4.66	5.37	6.57	7.79	9.47	10.82	13.34	16.22	18.15	21.06	23.68	26.87	29.14	36.12
15	5.23	5.98	7.26	8.55	10.31	11.72	14.34	17.32	19.31	22.31	25.00	28.26	30.58	37.70
16	5.81	6.61	7.96	9.31	11.15	12.62	15.34	18.42	20.46	23.54	26.30	29.63	32.00	39.29
17	6.41	7.26	8.67	10.08	12.00	13.53	16.34	19.51	21.62	24.77	27.59	31.00	33.41	40.75
18	7.02	7.91	9.39	10.86	12.86	14.44	17.34	20.60	22.76	25.99	28.87	32.35	34.80	42.31
19	7.63	8.57	10.12	11.65	13.72	15.35	18.34	21.69	23.90	27.20	30.14	33.69	36.19	43.82
20	8.26	9.24	10.85	12.44	14.58	16.27	19.34	22.78	25.04	28.41	31.41	35.02	37.57	45.32
21	8.90	9.92	11.59	13.24	15.44	17.18	20.34	23.86	26.17	29.62	32.67	36.34	38.93	46.80
22	9.54	10.60	12.34	14.04	16.31	18.10	21.24	24.94	27.30	30.81	33.92	37.66	40.29	48.27
23	10.20	11.29	13.09	14.85	17.19	19.02	22.34	26.02	28.43	32.01	35.17	38.97	41.64	49.73
24	10.86	11.99	13.85	15.66	18.06	19.94	23.34	27.10	29.55	33.20	36.42	40.27	42.98	51.18
25	11.52	12.70	14.61	16.47	18.94	20.87	24.34	28.17	30.68	34.38	37.65	41.57	44.31	52.62
26	12.20	13.41	15.38	17.29	19.82	21.79	25.34	29.25	31.80	35.56	38.88	42.86	45.64	54.05
27	12.88	14.12	16.15	18.11	20.70	22.72	26.34	30.32	32.91	36.74	40.11	44.14	46.96	55.48
28	13.56	14.85	16.93	18.94	21.59	23.65	27.34	31.39	34.03	37.92	41.34	45.42	48.28	56.89
29	14.26	15.57	17.71	19.77	22.48	24.58	28.34	32.46	35.14	39.09	42.56	46.69	49.59	58.30
30	14.95	16.31	18.49	20.60	23.36	25.51	29.34	33.53	36.25	40.26	43.77	47.96	50.89	59.70

Probability under H_0 that $\chi^2 \geq$ chi square

Table C. Table of Critical Values of T in the Wilcoxon Matched-Pairs Signed-Ranks Test

N	Level of significance for one-tailed test		
	.025	.01	.005
	Level of significance for two-tailed test		
	.05	.02	.01
6	0	—	—
7	2	0	—
8	4	2	0
9	6	3	2
10	8	5	3
11	11	7	5
12	14	10	7
13	17	13	10
14	21	16	13
15	25	20	16
16	30	24	20
17	35	28	23
18	40	33	28
19	46	38	32
20	52	43	38
21	59	49	43
22	66	56	49
23	73	62	55
24	81	69	61
25	89	77	68

Table C is adapted from Table I of Wilcoxon, F. 1949 (revised, 1964). *Some Rapid Approximate Statistical Procedures.* New York: American Cyanamid Company, p. 13, with the kind permission of the author and publisher.

APPENDIX

Table D. Table of Probabilities Associated with Values as Small as Observed Values of U in the Mann-Whitney Test

$n_2 = 3$

U \ n_1	1	2	3
0	.250	.100	.050
1	.500	.200	.100
2	.750	.400	.200
3		.600	.350
4			.500
5			.650

$n_2 = 4$

U \ n_1	1	2	3	4
0	.200	.067	.028	.014
1	.400	.133	.057	.029
2	.600	.267	.114	.057
3		.400	.200	.100
4		.600	.314	.171
5			.429	.243
6			.571	.343
7				.443
8				.557

$n_2 = 5$

U \ n_1	1	2	3	4	5
0	.167	.047	.018	.008	.004
1	.333	.095	.036	.016	.008
2	.500	.190	.071	.032	.016
3	.667	.286	.125	.056	.028
4		.429	.196	.095	.048
5		.571	.286	.143	.075
6			.393	.206	.111
7			.500	.278	.155
8			.607	.365	.210
9				.452	.274
10				.548	.345
11					.421
12					.500
13					.579

$n_2 = 6$

U \ n_1	1	2	3	4	5	6
0	.143	.036	.012	.005	.002	.001
1	.286	.071	.024	.010	.004	.002
2	.428	.143	.048	.019	.009	.004
3	.571	.214	.083	.033	.015	.008
4		.321	.131	.057	.026	.013
5		.429	.190	.086	.041	.021
6		.571	.274	.129	.063	.032
7			.357	.176	.089	.047
8			.452	.238	.123	.066
9			.548	.305	.165	.090
10				.381	.214	.120
11				.457	.268	.155
12				.545	.331	.197
13					.396	.242
14					.465	.294
15					.535	.350
16						.409
17						.469
18						.531

Reproduced from Mann, H.B., and Whitney, D.R. (1947). On a test of whether one of two random variables is stochastically larger than the other two. *Ann. Math. Statist.*, 18, pp. 52-54, with the kind permission of the authors and the publisher.

APPENDIX

Table D. Table of Probabilities Associated with Values as Small as Observed Values of *U* in the Mann-Whitney Test (*Continued*)

$n_2 = 7$

U \ n₁	1	2	3	4	5	6	7
0	.125	.028	.008	.003	.001	.001	.000
1	.250	.056	.017	.006	.003	.001	.001
2	.375	.111	.033	.012	.005	.002	.001
3	.500	.167	.058	.021	.009	.004	.002
4	.625	.250	.092	.036	.015	.007	.003
5		.333	.133	.055	.024	.011	.006
6		.444	.192	.082	.037	.017	.009
7		.556	.258	.115	.053	.026	.013
8			.333	.158	.074	.037	.019
9			.417	.206	.101	.051	.027
10			.500	.264	.134	.069	.036
11			.583	.324	.172	.090	.049
12				.394	.216	.117	.064
13				.464	.265	.147	.082
14				.538	.319	.183	.104
15					.378	.223	.130
16					.438	.267	.159
17					.500	.314	.191
18					.562	.365	.228
19						.418	.267
20						.473	.310
21						.527	.355
22							.402
23							.451
24							.500
25							.549

$n_2 = 8$

U \ n₁	1	2	3	4	5	6	7	8	t	Normal
0	.111	.022	.006	.002	.001	.000	.000	.000	3.308	.001
1	.222	.044	.012	.004	.002	.001	.000	.000	3.203	.001
2	.333	.089	.024	.008	.003	.001	.001	.000	3.098	.001
3	.444	.133	.042	.014	.005	.002	.001	.001	2.993	.001
4	.556	.200	.067	.024	.009	.004	.002	.001	2.888	.002
5		.267	.097	.036	.015	.006	.003	.001	2.783	.003
6		.356	.139	.055	.023	.010	.005	.002	2.678	.004
7		.444	.188	.077	.033	.015	.007	.003	2.573	.005
8		.556	.248	.107	.047	.021	.010	.005	2.468	.007
9			.315	.141	.064	.030	.014	.007	2.363	.009
10			.387	.184	.085	.041	.020	.010	2.258	.012
11			.461	.230	.111	.054	.027	.014	2.153	.016
12			.539	.285	.142	.071	.036	.019	2.048	.020
13				.341	.177	.091	.047	.025	1.943	.026
14				.404	.217	.114	.060	.032	1.838	.033
15				.467	.262	.141	.076	.041	1.733	.041
16				.533	.311	.172	.095	.052	1.628	.052
17					.362	.207	.116	.065	1.523	.064
18					.416	.245	.140	.080	1.418	.078
19					.472	.286	.168	.097	1.313	.094
20					.528	.331	.198	.117	1.208	.113
21						.377	.232	.139	1.102	.135
22						.426	.268	.164	.998	.159
23						.475	.306	.191	.893	.185
24						.525	.347	.221	.788	.215
25							.389	.253	.683	.247
26							.433	.287	.578	.282
27							.478	.323	.473	.318
28							.522	.360	.368	.356
29								.399	.263	.396
30								.439	.158	.437
31								.480	.052	.481
32								.520		

Table D is reproduced from Mann, H.B., and Whitney, D.R. (1947). On a test of whether one of two random variables is stochastically larger than the other two. *Ann. Math. Statist.*, 18, pp. 52-54, with the kind permission of the authors and the publisher.

APPENDIX

Table D. Table of Critical Values of U in the Mann-Whitney Test

Critical Values of U for a One-tailed Test at $\alpha = .001$ or for a Two-tailed Test at $\alpha = .002$

n_1 \ n_2	9	10	11	12	13	14	15	16	17	18	19	20
1												
2												
3									0	0	0	0
4		0	0	0	1	1	1	2	2	3	3	3
5	1	1	2	2	3	3	4	5	5	6	7	7
6	2	3	4	4	5	6	7	8	9	10	11	12
7	3	5	6	7	8	9	10	11	13	14	15	16
8	5	6	8	9	11	12	14	15	17	18	20	21
9	7	8	10	12	14	15	17	19	21	23	25	26
10	8	10	12	14	17	19	21	23	25	27	29	32
11	10	12	15	17	20	22	24	27	29	32	34	37
12	12	14	17	20	23	25	28	31	34	37	40	42
13	14	17	20	23	26	29	32	35	38	42	45	48
14	15	19	23	25	29	32	36	39	43	46	50	54
15	17	21	25	28	32	36	40	43	47	51	55	59
16	19	23	27	31	35	39	43	48	52	56	60	65
17	21	25	29	34	38	43	47	52	57	61	66	70
18	23	27	32	37	42	46	51	56	61	66	71	76
19	25	29	34	40	45	50	55	60	66	71	77	82
20	26	32	37	42	48	54	59	65	70	76	82	88

Table K_{II}. Critical Values of U for a One-tailed Test at $\alpha = .01$ or for a Two-tailed Test at $\alpha = .02$

n_1 \ n_2	9	10	11	12	13	14	15	16	17	18	19	20
1												
2					0	0	0	0	0	0	1	1
3	1	1	1	2	2	2	3	3	4	4	4	5
4	3	3	4	5	5	6	7	7	8	9	9	10
5	5	6	7	8	9	10	11	12	13	14	15	16
6	7	8	9	11	12	13	15	16	18	19	20	22
7	9	11	12	14	16	17	19	21	23	24	26	28
8	11	13	15	17	20	22	24	26	28	30	32	34
9	14	16	18	21	23	26	28	31	33	36	38	40
10	16	19	22	24	27	30	33	36	38	41	44	47
11	18	22	25	28	31	34	37	41	44	47	50	53
12	21	24	28	31	35	38	42	46	49	53	56	60
13	23	27	31	35	39	43	47	51	55	59	63	67
14	26	30	34	38	43	47	51	56	60	65	69	73
15	28	33	37	42	47	51	56	61	66	70	75	80
16	31	36	41	46	51	56	61	66	71	76	82	87
17	33	38	44	49	55	60	66	71	77	82	88	93
18	36	41	47	53	59	65	70	76	82	88	94	100
19	38	44	50	56	63	69	75	82	88	94	101	107
20	40	47	53	60	67	73	80	87	93	100	107	114

The D Tables on this page are adapted and abridged from Tables 1, 3, 5, and 7 of Auble, D. 1953. Extended tables for the Mann-Whitney statistic. *Bulletin of the Institute of Educational Research at Indiana University*, 1, no. 2, with the kind permission of the author and the publisher.

APPENDIX

Table D. Table of Critical Values of U in the Mann-Whitney Test (Continued)

Table K$_{III}$: Critical Values of U for a One-tailed Test at α = .025 or for a Two-tailed Test at α = .05

n$_2$ \ n$_1$	9	10	11	12	13	14	15	16	17	18	19	20
1												
2	0	0	0	1	1	1	1	1	2	2	2	2
3	2	3	3	4	4	5	5	6	6	7	7	8
4	4	5	6	7	8	9	10	11	11	12	13	13
5	7	8	9	11	12	13	14	15	17	18	19	20
6	10	11	13	14	16	17	19	21	22	24	25	27
7	12	14	16	18	20	22	24	26	28	30	32	34
8	15	17	19	22	24	26	29	31	34	36	38	41
9	17	20	23	26	28	31	34	37	39	42	45	48
10	20	23	26	29	33	36	39	42	45	48	52	55
11	23	26	30	33	37	40	44	47	51	55	58	62
12	26	29	33	37	41	45	49	53	57	61	65	69
13	28	33	37	41	45	50	54	59	63	67	72	76
14	31	36	40	45	50	55	59	64	67	74	78	83
15	34	39	44	49	54	59	64	70	75	80	85	90
16	37	42	47	53	59	64	70	75	81	86	92	98
17	39	45	51	57	63	67	75	81	87	93	99	105
18	42	48	55	61	67	74	80	86	93	99	106	112
19	45	52	58	65	72	78	85	92	99	106	113	119
20	48	55	62	69	76	83	90	98	105	112	119	127

Table K$_{IV}$: Critical Values of U for a One-tailed Test at α = .05 or for a One-tailed Test at α = .10

n$_2$ \ n$_1$	9	10	11	12	13	14	15	16	17	18	19	20
1												0
2	1	1	1	2	2	2	3	3	3	4	4	4
3	3	4	5	5	6	7	7	8	9	9	10	11
4	6	7	8	9	10	11	12	14	15	16	17	18
5	9	11	12	13	15	16	18	19	20	22	23	25
6	12	14	16	17	19	21	23	25	26	28	30	32
7	15	17	19	21	24	26	28	30	33	35	37	39
8	18	20	23	26	28	31	33	36	39	41	44	47
9	21	24	27	30	33	36	39	42	45	48	51	54
10	24	27	31	34	37	41	44	48	51	55	58	62
11	27	31	34	38	42	46	50	54	57	61	65	69
12	30	34	38	42	47	51	55	60	64	68	72	77
13	33	37	42	47	51	56	61	65	70	75	80	84
14	36	41	46	51	56	61	66	71	77	82	87	92
15	39	44	50	55	61	66	72	77	83	88	94	100
16	42	48	54	60	65	71	77	83	89	95	101	107
17	45	51	57	64	70	77	83	89	96	102	109	115
18	48	55	61	68	75	82	88	95	102	109	116	123
19	51	58	65	72	80	87	94	101	109	116	123	130
20	54	62	69	77	84	92	100	107	115	123	130	138

The D Tables on this page are adapted and abridged from Tables 1, 3, 5, and 7 of Auble, D. 1953. Extended tables for the Mann-Whitney statistic. *Bulletin of the Institute of Educational Research at Indiana University*, 1, No. 2, with the kind permission of the author and the publisher.

APPENDIX

Table E. Table of Probabilities Associated with Values as Large as Observed Values of χ_r^2 in the Friedman Two-Way Analysis of Variance by Ranks

Table N_I. $k = 3$

$N = 2$		$N = 3$		$N = 4$		$N = 5$	
χ_r^2	p	χ_r^2	p	χ_r^2	p	χ_r^2	p
0	1.000	.000	1.000	.0	1.000	.0	1.000
1	.833	.667	.944	.5	.931	.4	.954
3	.500	2.000	.528	1.5	.653	1.2	.691
4	.167	2.667	.361	2.0	.431	1.6	.522
		4.667	.194	3.5	.273	2.8	.367
		6.000	.028	4.5	.125	3.6	.182
				6.0	.069	4.8	.124
				6.5	.042	5.2	.093
				8.0	.0046	6.4	.039
						7.6	.024
						8.4	.0085
						10.0	.00077

$N = 6$		$N = 7$		$N = 8$		$N = 9$	
χ_r^2	p	χ_r^2	p	χ_r^2	p	χ_r^2	p
.00	1.000	.000	1.000	.00	1.000	.000	1.000
.33	.956	.286	.964	.25	.967	.222	.971
1.00	.740	.857	.768	.75	.794	.667	.814
1.33	.570	1.143	.620	1.00	.654	.889	.865
2.33	.430	2.000	.486	1.75	.531	1.556	.569
3.00	.252	2.571	.305	2.25	.355	2.000	.398
4.00	.184	3.429	.237	3.00	.285	2.667	.328
4.33	.142	3.714	.192	3.25	.236	2.889	.278
5.33	.072	4.571	.112	4.00	.149	3.556	.187
6.33	.052	5.429	.085	4.75	.120	4.222	.154
7.00	.029	6.000	.052	5.25	.079	4.667	.107
8.33	.012	7.143	.027	6.25	.047	5.556	.069
9.00	.0081	7.714	.021	6.75	.038	6.000	.057
9.33	.0055	8.000	.016	7.00	.030	6.222	.048
10.33	.0017	8.857	.0084	7.75	.018	6.889	.031
12.00	.00013	10.286	.0036	9.00	.0099	8.000	.019
		10.571	.0027	9.25	.0080	8.222	.016
		11.143	.0012	9.75	.0048	8.667	.010
		12.286	.00032	10.75	.0024	9.556	.0060
		14.000	.000021	12.00	.0011	10.667	.0035
				12.25	.00086	10.889	.0029
				13.00	.00026	11.556	.0013
				14.25	.000061	12.667	.00066
				16.00	.0000036	13.556	.00035
						14.000	.00020
						14.222	.000097
						14.889	.000054
						16.222	.000011
						18.000	.0000006

Table N_{II}. $k = 4$

$N = 2$		$N = 3$		$N = 4$		$N = 4$	
χ_r^2	p	χ_r^2	p	χ_r^2	p	χ_r^2	p
.0	1.000	.2	1.000	.0	1.000	5.7	.141
.6	.958	.6	.958	.3	.992	6.0	.105
1.2	.834	1.0	.910	.6	.928	6.3	.094
1.8	.792	1.8	.727	.9	.900	6.6	.077
2.4	.625	2.2	.608	1.2	.800	6.9	.068
3.0	.542	2.6	.524	1.5	.754	7.2	.054
3.6	.458	3.4	.446	1.8	.677	7.5	.052
4.2	.375	3.8	.342	2.1	.649	7.8	.036
4.8	.208	4.2	.300	2.4	.524	8.1	.033
5.4	.167	5.0	.207	2.7	.508	8.4	.019
6.0	.042	5.4	.175	3.0	.432	8.7	.014
		5.8	.148	3.3	.389	9.3	.012
		6.6	.075	3.6	.355	9.6	.0069
		7.0	.054	3.9	.324	9.9	.0062
		7.4	.033	4.5	.242	10.2	.0027
		8.2	.017	4.8	.200	10.8	.0016
		9.0	.0017	5.1	.190	11.1	.00094
				5.4	.158	12.0	.000072

Tables E are adapted from Friedman, M. 1937. The use of ranks to avoid the assumption of normality implicit in the analysis of variance. *J. Amer. Statist. Ass*, 32, **688-689**, with the kind permission of the author and the publisher.

Table F. Table of Probabilities Associated with Values as Large as Observed Values of H in the Kruskal-Wallis One-Way Analysis of Variance by Ranks*

n_1	n_2	n_3	H	p	n_1	n_2	n_3	H	p
2	1	1	2.7000	.500	4	3	2	6.4444	.008
								6.3000	.011
2	2	1	3.6000	.200				5.4444	.046
								5.4000	.051
2	2	2	4.5714	.067				4.5111	.098
			3.7143	.200				4.4444	.102
3	1	1	3.2000	.300	4	3	3	6.7455	.010
3	2	1	4.2857	.100				6.7091	.013
			3.8571	.133				5.7909	.046
3	2	2	5.3572	.029				5.7273	.050
			4.7143	.048				4.7091	.092
			4.5000	.067				4.7000	.101
			4.4643	.105	4	4	1	6.6667	.010
3	3	1	5.1429	.043				6.1667	.022
			4.5714	.100				4.9667	.048
			4.0000	.129				4.8667	.054
3	3	2	6.2500	.011				4.1667	.082
			5.3611	.032				4.0667	.102
			5.1389	.061	4	4	2	7.0364	.006
			4.5556	.100				6.8727	.011
			4.2500	.121				5.4545	.046
3	3	3	7.2000	.004				5.2364	.052
			6.4889	.011				4.5545	.098
			5.6889	.029				4.4455	.103
			5.6000	.050	4	4	3	7.1439	.010
			5.0667	.086				7.1364	.011
			4.6222	.100				5.5985	.049
4	1	1	3.5714	.200				5.5758	.051
4	2	1	4.8214	.057				4.5455	.099
			4.5000	.076				4.4773	.102
			4.0179	.114	4	4	4	7.6538	.008
4	2	2	6.0000	.014				7.5385	.011
			5.3333	.033				5.6923	.049
			5.1250	.052				5.6538	.054
			4.4583	.100				4.6539	.097
			4.1667	.105				4.5001	.104
4	3	1	5.8333	.021	5	1	1	3.8571	.143
			5.2083	.050	5	2	1	5.2500	.036
			5.0000	.057				5.0000	.048
			4.0556	.093				4.4500	.071
			3.8889	.129				4.2000	.095
								4.0500	.119

Table F adapted and abridged from Kruskal, W.H., and Wallis, W.A. 1952. Use of ranks in one-criterion variance analysis. *J. Am. Stat. Ass.* permission.

Table F. Table of Probabilities Associated with Values as Large as Observed Values of H in the Kruskal-Wallis One-way Analysis of Variance by Ranks (continued)

n_1	n_2	n_3	H	p	n_1	n_2	n_3	H	p
5	2	2	6.5333	.008				5.6308	.050
			6.1333	.013				4.5487	.099
			5.1600	.034				4.5231	.103
			5.0400	.056	5	4	4	7.7604	.009
			4.3733	.090				7.7440	.011
			4.2933	.122				5.6571	.049
5	3	1	6.4000	.012				5.6176	.050
			4.9600	.048				4.6187	.100
			4.8711	.052				4.5527	.102
			4.0178	.095	5	5	1	7.3091	.009
			3.8400	.123				6.8364	.011
5	3	2	6.9091	.009				5.1273	.046
			6.8218	.010				4.9091	.053
			5.2509	.049				4.1091	.086
			5.1055	.052				4.0364	.105
			4.6509	.091	5	5	2	7.3385	.010
			4.4945	.101				7.2692	.010
5	3	3	7.0788	.009				5.3385	.047
			6.9818	.011				5.2462	.051
			5.6485	.049				4.6231	.097
			5.5152	.051				4.5077	.100
			4.5333	.097	5	5	3	7.5780	.010
			4.4121	.109				7.5429	.010
5	4	1	6.9545	.008				5.7055	.046
			6.8400	.011				5.6264	.051
			4.9855	.044				4.5451	.100
			4.8600	.056				4.5363	.102
			3.9873	.098	5	5	4	7.8229	.010
			3.9600	.102				7.7914	.010
5	4	2	7.2045	.009				5.6657	.049
			7.1182	.010				5.6429	.050
			5.2727	.049				4.5229	.099
			5.2682	.050				4.5200	.101
			4.5409	.098	5	5	5	8.0000	.009
			4.5182	.101				7.9800	.010
5	4	3	7.4449	.010				5.7800	.049
			7.3949	.011				5.6600	.051
			5.6564	.049				4.5600	.100
								4.5000	.102

Table F adapted and abridged from Kruskal, W.H., and Wallis, W.A. 1952. Use of ranks in one-criterion variance analysis. *J. Am. Stat. Ass.* permission.

Table G. Table of Critical Values of *t*

df	|	|	|	|	|	|
	Level of significance for one-tailed test					
	.10	.05	.025	.01	.005	.0005
	Level of significance for two-tailed test					
	.20	.10	.05	.02	.01	.001
1	3.078	6.314	12.706	31.821	63.657	636.619
2	1.886	2.920	4.303	6.965	9.925	31.598
3	1.638	2.353	3.182	4.541	5.841	12.941
4	1.533	2.132	2.776	3.747	4.604	8.610
5	1.476	2.015	2.571	3.365	4.032	6.859
6	1.440	1.943	2.447	3.143	3.707	5.959
7	1.415	1.895	2.365	2.998	3.499	5.405
8	1.397	1.860	2.306	2.896	3.355	5.041
9	1.383	1.833	2.262	2.821	3.250	4.781
10	1.372	1.812	2.228	2.764	3.169	4.587
11	1.363	1.796	2.201	2.718	3.106	4.437
12	1.356	1.782	2.179	2.681	3.055	4.318
13	1.350	1.771	2.160	2.650	3.012	4.221
14	1.345	1.761	2.145	2.624	2.977	4.140
15	1.341	1.753	2.131	2.602	2.947	4.073
16	1.337	1.746	2.120	2.583	2.921	4.015
17	1.333	1.740	2.110	2.567	2.898	3.965
18	1.330	1.734	2.101	2.552	2.878	3.922
19	1.328	1.729	2.093	2.539	2.861	3.883
20	1.325	1.725	2.086	2.528	2.845	3.850
21	1.323	1.721	2.080	2.518	2.831	3.819
22	1.321	1.717	2.074	2.508	2.819	3.792
23	1.319	1.714	2.069	2.500	2.807	3.767
24	1.318	1.711	2.064	2.492	2.797	3.745
25	1.316	1.708	2.060	2.485	2.787	3.725
26	1.315	1.706	2.056	2.479	2.779	3.707
27	1.314	1.703	2.052	2.473	2.771	3.690
28	1.313	1.701	2.048	2.467	2.763	3.674
29	1.311	1.699	2.045	2.462	2.756	3.659
30	1.310	1.697	2.042	2.457	2.750	3.646
40	1.303	1.684	2.021	2.423	2.704	3.551
60	1.296	1.671	2.000	2.390	2.660	3.460
120	1.289	1.658	1.980	2.358	2.617	3.373
∞	1.282	1.645	1.960	2.326	2.576	3.291

Table G is taken from Table III of Fisher and Yates: *Statistical Tables for Biological, Agricultural and Medical Research*, 6th edition, 1963, published by Oliver and Boyd, Edinburgh, and by permission of the authors and publishers.

Table H
Percentage Points of the F Distribution
Upper 5% Points

$\nu_2 \backslash \nu_1$	1	2	3	4	5	6	7	8	9	10	12	15	20	24	30	40	60	120	∞
1	161.4	199.5	215.7	224.6	230.2	234.0	236.8	238.9	240.5	241.9	243.9	245.9	248.0	249.1	250.1	251.1	252.2	253.3	254.3
2	18.51	19.00	19.16	19.25	19.30	19.33	19.35	19.37	19.38	19.40	19.41	19.43	19.45	19.45	19.46	19.47	19.48	19.49	19.50
3	10.13	9.55	9.28	9.12	9.01	8.94	8.89	8.85	8.81	8.79	8.74	8.70	8.66	8.64	8.62	8.59	8.57	8.55	8.53
4	7.71	6.94	6.59	6.39	6.26	6.16	6.09	6.04	6.00	5.96	5.91	5.86	5.80	5.77	5.75	5.72	5.69	5.66	5.63
5	6.61	5.79	5.41	5.19	5.05	4.95	4.88	4.82	4.77	4.74	4.68	4.62	4.56	4.53	4.50	4.46	4.43	4.40	4.36
6	5.99	5.14	4.76	4.53	4.39	4.28	4.21	4.15	4.10	4.06	4.00	3.94	3.87	3.84	3.81	3.77	3.74	3.70	3.67
7	5.59	4.74	4.35	4.12	3.97	3.87	3.79	3.73	3.68	3.64	3.57	3.51	3.44	3.41	3.38	3.34	3.30	3.27	3.23
8	5.32	4.46	4.07	3.84	3.69	3.58	3.50	3.44	3.39	3.35	3.28	3.22	3.15	3.12	3.08	3.04	3.01	2.97	2.93
9	5.12	4.26	3.86	3.63	3.48	3.37	3.29	3.23	3.18	3.14	3.07	3.01	2.94	2.90	2.86	2.83	2.79	2.75	2.71
10	4.96	4.10	3.71	3.48	3.33	3.22	3.14	3.07	3.02	2.98	2.91	2.85	2.77	2.74	2.70	2.66	2.62	2.58	2.54
11	4.84	3.98	3.59	3.36	3.20	3.09	3.01	2.95	2.90	2.85	2.79	2.72	2.65	2.61	2.57	2.53	2.49	2.45	2.40
12	4.75	3.89	3.49	3.26	3.11	3.00	2.91	2.85	2.80	2.75	2.69	2.62	2.54	2.51	2.47	2.43	2.38	2.34	2.30
13	4.67	3.81	3.41	3.18	3.03	2.92	2.83	2.77	2.71	2.67	2.60	2.53	2.46	2.42	2.38	2.34	2.30	2.25	2.21
14	4.60	3.74	3.34	3.11	2.96	2.85	2.76	2.70	2.65	2.60	2.53	2.46	2.39	2.35	2.31	2.27	2.22	2.18	2.13
15	4.54	3.68	3.29	3.06	2.90	2.79	2.71	2.64	2.59	2.54	2.48	2.40	2.33	2.29	2.25	2.20	2.16	2.11	2.07
16	4.49	3.63	3.24	3.01	2.85	2.74	2.66	2.59	2.54	2.49	2.42	2.35	2.28	2.24	2.19	2.15	2.11	2.06	2.01
17	4.45	3.59	3.20	2.96	2.81	2.70	2.61	2.55	2.49	2.45	2.38	2.31	2.23	2.19	2.15	2.10	2.06	2.01	1.96
18	4.41	3.55	3.16	2.93	2.77	2.66	2.58	2.51	2.46	2.41	2.34	2.27	2.19	2.15	2.11	2.06	2.02	1.97	1.92
19	4.38	3.52	3.13	2.90	2.74	2.63	2.54	2.48	2.42	2.38	2.31	2.23	2.16	2.11	2.07	2.03	1.98	1.93	1.88
20	4.35	3.49	3.10	2.87	2.71	2.60	2.51	2.45	2.39	2.35	2.28	2.20	2.12	2.08	2.04	1.99	1.95	1.90	1.84
21	4.32	3.47	3.07	2.84	2.68	2.57	2.49	2.42	2.37	2.32	2.25	2.18	2.10	2.05	2.01	1.96	1.92	1.87	1.81
22	4.30	3.44	3.05	2.82	2.66	2.55	2.46	2.40	2.34	2.30	2.23	2.15	2.07	2.03	1.98	1.94	1.89	1.84	1.78
23	4.28	3.42	3.03	2.80	2.64	2.53	2.44	2.37	2.32	2.27	2.20	2.13	2.05	2.01	1.96	1.91	1.86	1.81	1.76
24	4.26	3.40	3.01	2.78	2.62	2.51	2.42	2.36	2.30	2.25	2.18	2.11	2.03	1.98	1.94	1.89	1.84	1.79	1.73
25	4.24	3.39	2.99	2.76	2.60	2.49	2.40	2.34	2.28	2.24	2.16	2.09	2.01	1.96	1.92	1.87	1.82	1.77	1.71
26	4.23	3.37	2.98	2.74	2.59	2.47	2.39	2.32	2.27	2.22	2.15	2.07	1.99	1.95	1.90	1.85	1.80	1.75	1.69
27	4.21	3.35	2.96	2.73	2.57	2.46	2.37	2.31	2.25	2.20	2.13	2.06	1.97	1.93	1.88	1.84	1.79	1.73	1.67
28	4.20	3.34	2.95	2.71	2.56	2.45	2.36	2.29	2.24	2.19	2.12	2.04	1.96	1.91	1.87	1.82	1.77	1.71	1.65
29	4.18	3.33	2.93	2.70	2.55	2.43	2.35	2.28	2.22	2.18	2.10	2.03	1.94	1.90	1.85	1.81	1.75	1.70	1.64
30	4.17	3.32	2.92	2.69	2.53	2.42	2.33	2.27	2.21	2.16	2.09	2.01	1.93	1.89	1.84	1.79	1.74	1.68	1.62
40	4.08	3.23	2.84	2.61	2.45	2.34	2.25	2.18	2.12	2.08	2.00	1.92	1.84	1.79	1.74	1.69	1.64	1.58	1.51
60	4.00	3.15	2.76	2.53	2.37	2.25	2.17	2.10	2.04	1.99	1.92	1.84	1.75	1.70	1.65	1.59	1.53	1.47	1.39
120	3.92	3.07	2.68	2.45	2.29	2.17	2.09	2.02	1.96	1.91	1.83	1.75	1.66	1.61	1.55	1.50	1.43	1.35	1.25
∞	3.84	3.00	2.60	2.37	2.21	2.10	2.01	1.94	1.88	1.83	1.75	1.67	1.57	1.52	1.46	1.39	1.32	1.22	1.00

Table I. Table of Critical Values of r_S, the Spearman Rank Correlation Coefficient

N	Significance level (one-tailed test)	
	.05	.01
4	1.000	
5	.900	1.000
6	.829	.943
7	.714	.893
8	.643	.833
9	.600	.783
10	.564	.746
12	.506	.712
14	.456	.645
16	.425	.601
18	.399	.564
20	.377	.534
22	359	.508
24	.343	.485
26	.329	.465
28	.317	.448
30	.306	.432

Table I adapted from Olds, E.G. 1938. Distributions of sums of squares of rank differences for small numbers of individuals. *Ann. Math. Statist.*, 9, 133-148, and 20, 117-118, (1949), with the kind permission of the author and the publisher.

Table J

Distribution of the Studentized Range Statistic

df for $s_{\bar{Y}}$	$1 - \alpha$	\multicolumn{14}{c}{Number of steps between ordered means}
		2	3	4	5	6	7	8	9	10	11	12	13	14	15
1	.95	18.0	27.0	32.8	37.1	40.4	43.1	45.4	47.4	49.1	50.6	52.0	53.2	54.3	55.4
	.99	90.0	135	164	186	202	216	227	237	246	253	260	266	272	277
2	.95	6.09	8.3	9.8	10.9	11.7	12.4	13.0	13.5	14.0	14.4	14.7	15.1	15.4	15.7
	.99	14.0	19.0	22.3	24.7	26.6	28.2	29.5	30.7	31.7	32.6	33.4	34.1	34.8	35.4
3	.95	4.50	5.91	6.82	7.50	8.04	8.48	8.85	9.18	9.46	9.72	9.95	10.2	10.4	10.5
	.99	8.26	10.6	12.2	13.3	14.2	15.0	15.6	16.2	16.7	17.1	17.5	17.9	18.2	18.5
4	.95	3.93	5.04	5.76	6.29	6.71	7.05	7.35	7.60	7.83	8.03	8.21	8.37	8.52	8.66
	.99	6.51	8.12	9.17	9.96	10.6	11.1	11.5	11.9	12.3	12.6	12.8	13.1	13.3	13.5
5	.95	3.64	4.60	5.22	5.67	6.03	6.33	6.58	6.80	6.99	7.17	7.32	7.47	7.60	7.72
	.99	5.70	6.97	7.80	8.42	8.91	9.32	9.67	9.97	10.2	10.5	10.7	10.9	11.1	11.2
6	.95	3.46	4.34	4.90	5.31	5.63	5.89	6.12	6.32	6.49	6.65	6.79	6.92	7.03	7.14
	.99	5.24	6.33	7.03	7.56	7.97	8.32	8.61	8.87	9.10	9.30	9.49	9.65	9.81	9.95
7	.95	3.34	4.16	4.69	5.06	5.36	5.61	5.82	6.00	6.16	6.30	6.43	6.55	6.66	6.76
	.99	4.95	5.92	6.54	7.01	7.37	7.68	7.94	8.17	8.37	8.55	8.71	8.86	9.00	9.12
8	.95	3.26	4.04	4.53	4.89	5.17	5.40	5.60	5.77	5.92	6.05	6.18	6.29	6.39	6.48
	.99	4.74	5.63	6.20	6.63	6.96	7.24	7.47	7.68	7.87	8.03	8.18	8.31	8.44	8.55
9	.95	3.20	3.95	4.42	4.76	5.02	5.24	5.43	5.60	5.74	5.87	5.98	6.09	6.19	6.28
	.99	4.60	5.43	5.96	6.35	6.66	6.91	7.13	7.32	7.49	7.65	7.78	7.91	8.03	8.13
10	.95	3.15	3.88	4.33	4.65	4.91	5.12	5.30	5.46	5.60	5.72	5.83	5.93	6.03	6.11
	.99	4.48	5.27	5.77	6.14	6.43	6.67	6.87	7.05	7.21	7.36	7.48	7.60	7.71	7.81
11	.95	3.11	3.82	4.26	4.57	4.82	5.03	5.20	5.35	5.49	5.61	5.71	5.81	5.90	5.99
	.99	4.39	5.14	5.62	5.97	6.25	6.48	6.67	6.84	6.99	7.13	7.26	7.36	7.46	7.56
12	.95	3.08	3.77	4.20	4.51	4.75	4.95	5.12	5.27	5.40	5.51	5.62	5.71	5.80	5.88
	.99	4.32	5.04	5.50	5.84	6.10	6.32	6.51	6.67	6.81	6.94	7.06	7.17	7.26	7.36
13	.95	3.06	3.73	4.15	4.45	4.69	4.88	5.05	5.19	5.32	5.43	5.53	5.63	5.71	5.79
	.99	4.26	4.96	5.40	5.73	5.98	6.19	6.37	6.53	6.67	6.79	6.90	7.01	7.10	7.19
14	.95	3.03	3.70	4.11	4.41	4.64	4.83	4.99	5.13	5.25	5.36	5.46	5.55	6.64	5.72
	.99	4.21	4.89	5.32	5.63	5.88	6.08	6.26	6.41	6.54	6.66	6.77	6.87	6.96	7.05
16	.95	3.00	3.65	4.05	4.33	4.56	4.74	4.90	5.03	5.15	5.26	5.35	5.44	5.52	5.59
	.99	4.13	4.78	5.19	5.49	5.72	5.92	6.08	6.22	6.35	6.46	6.56	6.66	6.74	6.82
18	.95	2.97	3.61	4.00	4.28	4.49	4.67	4.82	4.96	5.07	5.17	5.27	5.35	5.43	5.50
	.99	4.07	4.70	5.09	5.38	5.60	5.79	5.94	6.08	6.20	6.31	6.41	6.50	6.58	6.65
20	.95	2.95	3.58	3.96	4.23	4.45	4.62	4.77	4.90	5.01	5.11	5.20	5.28	5.36	5.43
	.99	4.02	4.64	5.02	5.29	5.51	5.69	5.84	5.97	6.09	6.19	6.29	6.37	6.45	6.52
24	.95	2.92	3.53	3.90	4.17	4.37	4.54	4.68	4.81	4.92	5.01	5.10	5.18	5.25	5.32
	.99	3.96	4.54	4.91	5.17	5.37	5.54	5.69	5.81	5.92	6.02	6.11	6.19	6.26	6.33
30	.95	2.89	3.49	3.84	4.10	4.30	4.46	4.60	4.72	4.83	4.92	5.00	5.08	5.15	5.21
	.99	3.89	4.45	4.80	5.05	5.24	5.40	5.54	5.56	5.76	5.85	5.93	6.01	6.08	6.14
40	.95	2.86	3.44	3.79	4.04	4.23	4.39	4.52	4.63	4.74	4.82	4.91	4.98	5.05	5.11
	.99	3.82	4.37	4.70	4.93	5.11	5.27	5.39	5.50	5.60	5.69	5.77	5.84	5.90	5.96
60	.95	2.83	3.40	3.74	3.98	4.16	4.31	4.44	4.55	4.65	4.73	4.81	4.88	4.94	5.00
	.99	3.76	4.28	4.60	4.82	4.99	5.13	5.25	5.36	5.45	5.53	5.60	5.67	5.73	5.79
120	.95	2.80	3.36	3.69	3.92	4.10	4.24	4.36	4.48	4.56	4.64	4.72	4.78	4.84	4.90
	.99	3.70	4.20	4.50	4.71	4.87	5.01	5.12	5.21	5.30	5.38	5.44	5.51	5.56	5.61
∞	.95	2.77	3.31	3.63	3.86	4.03	4.17	4.29	4.39	4.47	4.55	4.62	4.68	4.74	4.80
	.99	3.64	4.12	4.40	4.60	4.76	4.88	4.99	5.08	5.16	5.23	5.29	5.35	5.40	5.45

Table J is adapted from Table 11.2 in *The Probability Integrals of the Range and of the Studentized Range*, prepared by H.L. Harter, D.S. Clemm, and E.H. Guthrie. These tables are published in WADC tech. Rep. 58-484, vol. 2, 1959, Wright Air Development Center, and are used with kind permission of the authors.

PRE/POSTTEST TO PROGRAM I
A Programmed Guide to Closed Systems

1. Write the definition of a "closed system."

2. Since lemons, oranges, limes, and tangerines are all citrus fruits, they can be grouped together in what is called a _____ .

3. There are no cognates between English and Arabic, but 46% between English and French. Between English and French, _____ is easier.

4. Define "mode of inquiry" and list three (3) examples.

5. Name at least four closed systems which are used in reading and/or performing music from a musical score.

   a.

   b.

   c.

   d.

6. Draw a line from each term to its appropriate formula:

   Phenomenological

   Assumptive

   Hypothetical

   1. A ∴ B   C
   2. B / C   C
   3. (A) B = C
   4. A / B   C
   5. (A) B   C ∴ A
   6. B   C = A

7. List ten closed systems represented on this musical score:

   a.   e.   h.
   b.   f.   i.
   c.   g.   j.
   d.

STRING QUARTET NO. 16 IN F MAJOR, OPUS 135

Allegretto

Ludwig van Beethoven
(1826)

PRE/POSTTEST TO PROGRAM I
A Programmed Guide to Closed Systems

1. Write the definition of a "closed system."

2. Since lemons, oranges, limes, and tangerines are all citrus fruits, they can be grouped together in what is called a _____ .

3. There are no cognates between English and Arabic, but 46% between English and French. Between English and French, _____ is easier.

4. Define "mode of inquiry" and list three (3) examples.

5. Name at least four closed systems which are used in reading and/or performing music from a musical score.

   a.

   b.

   c.

   d.

6. Draw a line from each term to its appropriate formula:

Phenomenological		1.	A	∴	B		C	

   Phenomenological   1.   A ∴ B   C
                            2.   B / C   C
                            3.   (A)   B = C
   Assumptive   4.   A / B   C
                            5.   (A)   B   C ∴ A
   Hypothetical   6.   B   C = A

7. List ten closed systems represented on this musical score:

a.	e.	h.
b.	f.	i.
c.	g.	j.
d.		

STRING QUARTET NO. 16 IN F MAJOR, OPUS 135

Allegretto

Ludwig van Beethoven
(1826)

PRE/POSTTEST PROGRAM II
A Programmed Guide to Mill's Canons

1. Explain the origin of the Mill's Canons. _____
   _____
   _____

2. What is the rationale of the Mill's Canons? _____
   _____
   _____

3. Briefly explain the value of Mill's Canons to the music researcher. _____
   _____
   _____

4. Define Mill's Method of Agreement. _____
   _____
   _____

5. Define Mill's Method of Difference. _____
   _____
   _____

6. Define Mill's Joint Method. _____
   _____
   _____

7. Define Mill's Method of Residues. _____
   _____
   _____

8. Define Mill's Method of Concomitant Variation. _____
   _____
   _____

9. An experimenter evaluating the tone quality produced by using a Bach 7C mouthpiece sets up an experimental group using this mouthpiece and a control group using other trumpet mouthpieces. The only variable that is different in the experiment is the mouthpiece. This experiment is structured within which Mill's Canon? _____

10. Two trumpet players out of a group of five are able to play double high "C." The only thing that these two players have in common is that they both use Bach 7C mouthpieces. With all the other variables remaining stable, these two players try an assortment of mouthpieces to determine if indeed the only reason for their being able to play doubled high "C" is the use of a Bach 7C mouthpiece. Which Mill's Canon explains the structure of this experiment? _____

11. Two trumpet players out of a group of five are able to play double high "C." The only thing that these two players have in common is that they both use Bach 7C mouthpieces. The reason that they are able to play double high "C" is that they use Bach 7C mouthpieces. This event is explained by which Mill's Canon?_____

12. A trumpet player who practices twelve hours each week is able to play double high "C," but while preparing for final exams he is only able to practice six hours during a two week period. At the end of the two week period he is unable to produce a double high "C." This event is explained by which Mill's Canon? _____

13. It is concluded that a certain type of mouthpiece and a specific practice procedure will assist the trumpet player to produce double high "C." All other factors which are necessary for this production are unknown. This phenomonen is explained by which Mill's Canon?_____

MILL'S CANONS

A. Method of Agreement.
B. Method of Differences.
C. Joint Method.

D. Method of Residues.
E. Concomitant Variations.

Place the letter of canon used in the item in the space before the number.

1. A man is found dead on the streets of New York City. Police investigate and find that he did not die of natural causes. It must be something else.

2. Several murders had occurred in recent weeks, and only one factor was common to the technique of killing: stabbing with a mysterious sharp object. Police suspect the same killer is responsible.

3. Further investigation shows that the murders only occurred on bitter cold days. In a few days there occurred another bitter cold day and another identical murder. The police felt they were on to something.

4. Police noted that as there were more bitter cold days, there were more identical murders. The trail got hot (or was it cold?)

5. Lab tests revealed that the murder weapon was neither wood nor metal. The plot thickened. What was the murder weapon?

6. Police reasoned that the killer must be psychopathic because that kind of cruelty was only characteristic of psychopaths.

7. As spring approached and the number of bitter cold days declined, the mystery murders became fewer. By summer they had stopped.

8. One day the phone rang at police headquarters, and a voice said, "I want to give myself up. Please help me before winter comes again." The caller, as it turned out, confessed to the murders, supplying details that no other person could have known.

9. So the killer was kept in custody, and the streets were safe. But one bitter cold day he escaped, and there was another psycho murder.

10. As the police stepped up their attempts to catch him, the murderer increased his skill at eluding them.

11. At last the killer again gave up, telling police, "It was not a knife I used." Police reasoned it must have been something else.

12. "You see, it was an icicle," he said. Thus ended the saga, and people were no longer afraid to walk the streets on bitter cold days.

PRE/POSTTEST PROGRAM II
A Programmed Guide to Mill's Canons

1. Explain the origin of the Mill's Canons. _____
   _____
   _____

2. What is the rationale of the Mill's Canons? _____
   _____
   _____

3. Briefly explain the value of Mill's Canons to the music researcher. _____
   _____
   _____

4. Define Mill's Method of Agreement. _____
   _____
   _____

5. Define Mill's Method of Difference. _____
   _____
   _____

6. Define Mill's Joint Method. _____
   _____
   _____

7. Define Mill's Method of Residues. _____
   _____
   _____

8. Define Mill's Method of Concomitant Variation. _____
   _____
   _____

9. An experimenter evaluating the tone quality produced by using a Bach 7C mouthpiece sets up an experimental group using this mouthpiece and a control group using other trumpet mouthpieces. The only variable that is different in the experiment is the mouthpiece. This experiment is structured within which Mill's Canon? _____

10. Two trumpet players out of a group of five are able to play double high "C." The only thing that these two players have in common is that they both use Bach 7C mouthpieces. With all the other variables remaining stable, these two players try an assortment of mouthpieces to determine if indeed the only reason for their being able to play doubled high "C" is the use of a Bach 7C mouthpiece. Which Mill's Canon explains the structure of this experiment? _____

11. Two trumpet players out of a group of five are able to play double high "C." The only thing that these two players have in common is that they both use Bach 7C mouthpieces. The reason that they are able to play double high "C" is that they use Bach 7C mouthpieces. This event is

explained by which Mill's Canon?_____

12. A trumpet player who practices twelve hours each week is able to play double high "C," but while preparing for final exams he is only able to practice six hours during a two week period. At the end of the two week period he is unable to produce a double high "C." This event is

explained by which Mill's Canon? _____

13. It is concluded that a certain type of mouthpiece and a specific practice procedure will assist the trumpet player to produce double high "C." All other factors which are necessary for this

production are unknown. This phenomonen is explained by which Mill's Canon?_____

MILL'S CANONS

A. Method of Agreement.
B. Method of Differences.
C. Joint Method.

D. Method of Residues.
E. Concomitant Variations.

Place the letter of canon used in the item in the space before the number.

1. A man is found dead on the streets of New York City. Police investigate and find that he did not die of natural causes. It must be something else.

2. Several murders had occurred in recent weeks, and only one factor was common to the technique of killing: stabbing with a mysterious sharp object. Police suspect the same killer is responsible.

3. Further investigation shows that the murders only occurred on bitter cold days. In a few days there occurred another bitter cold day and another identical murder. The police felt they were on to something.

4. Police noted that as there were more bitter cold days, there were more identical murders. The trail got hot (or was it cold?)

5. Lab tests revealed that the murder weapon was neither wood nor metal. The plot thickened. What was the murder weapon?

6. Police reasoned that the killer must be psychopathic because that kind of cruelty was only characteristic of psychopaths.

7. As spring approached and the number of bitter cold days declined, the mystery murders became fewer. By summer they had stopped.

8. One day the phone rang at police headquarters, and a voice said, "I want to give myself up. Please help me before winter comes again." The caller, as it turned out, confessed to the murders, supplying details that no other person could have known.

9. So the killer was kept in custody, and the streets were safe. But one bitter cold day he escaped, and there was another psycho murder.

10. As the police stepped up their attempts to catch him, the murderer increased his skill at eluding them.

11. At last the killer again gave up, telling police, "It was not a knife I used." Police reasoned it must have been something else.

12. "You see, it was an icicle," he said. Thus ended the saga, and people were no longer afraid to walk the streets on bitter cold days.

PRE/POSTTEST TO PROGRAM III
A Programmed Guide to Selected Research Designs

NOTE: The seven (7) sample studies referred to in this test are found at the end of the test.

1. Match the appropriate type of samples with the type of samples used in each study.

   Study 1 _____

   Study 2 _____   a.   one-sample

   Study 3 _____   b.   two-sample, equivalent

   Study 4 _____   c.   two-sample, independent

   Study 5 _____   d.   multiple-sample, equivalent

   Study 6 _____   e.   multiple-sample, independent

   Study 7 _____

2. Write the symbols for:

   _____ treatment   _____ matching

   _____ measurement, or observation

3. Write in symbols the appropriate sequence of measurements and treatments used in the following studies:

   Study 1 _____   Study 6 _____

   Study 2 _____   Study 7 _____

   Study 3 _____

4. Match the appropriate level of measurement with the description of data given in each study:

   Study 1 _____   Study 6 _____

   Study 2 _____   Study 7 _____

   Study 3 _____   a.   nominal

   Study 4 _____   b.   ordinal

   Study 5 _____   c.   interval or ratio

5. Match an appropriate statistical test with the data described in each study:

   Study 1 _____   a. χ^2—*One Sample* test, especially good for data at nominal level.

   Study 2 _____

   Study 4 _____   b.   *McNemar Test for Sig. of Changes*, for use with two, equiv. samples when data are at nominal level.

   Study 6 _____

   Study 7 _____   c.   *Friedman Two-Way Analysis of Variance*, for multiple, equiv. samples—ordinal level.

   d.   *Mann-Whitney U*, two indep. samples, ordinal level.

   e.   *Parametric t-test*, one or two equiv. or indep. samples, data at the interval or ratio level.

145

6. Match the correct type of hypothesis with those given in the studies below:

Study 1 _____

Study 3 _____   a.   one-tailed alternative hypothesis.

Study 4 _____   b.   two-tailed alternative hypothesis.

Study 5 _____   c.   Null Hypothesis.

Study 7 _____

7. Write a two-tailed alternative hypothesis for Study *2*:

_____

_____

_____

8. Write a one-tailed alternative hypothesis for Study *6:*

_____

_____

_____

9. Write a Null Hypothesis for Study *3*:

_____

_____

_____

10. Choose a significance level for Study *7.* Write the symbol and definition of significance level, and the rationale for your choice.

symbol for significance level = _____

significance level chosen = _____

definition of significance level:_____

_____

_____

Rationale for choice:_____

_____

_____

Studies

STUDY 1: N = 30, total number of subjects

This study attempts to determine which element of music is *cited* as reason for liking the piece of music on first hearing. 30 students listened to a piece of music and indicated their choice of tempo, rhythm, beat, melody, *or* form as their reason for liking the music.

H_o: The two groups are from the same population and there is no difference in the expected number of responses falling into each category.

STUDY 2: N = 24, total number of subjects

24 subjects received pretest, were matched on the basis of this and divided into two groups. Group 1 (12 subjects) received instruction about a new piece of music and a posttest. Group 2 (12 subjects) received no instruction and a posttest. The pre- and posttests were behavioral observations of whether the subjects were "on task" (+) or "off task" (−). The experimenter was interested in the effect of *analytical music instruction* about a new piece of music on the "on-off task" behavior of subjects listening to that piece of music.

H_o: The two groups are from the same population and there will be no difference in the mean amount of "on-task" behavior demonstrated.

STUDY 3: N = 16, the total number of subjects

This study was designed to evaluate programmed lessons in score reading. Eight subjects were used as a no-contact control group receiving no instruction in score reading. Eight subjects were used as an experimental group and read the programmed instruction in score reading. All 16 subjects were given a posttest consisting of a pass (+) or fail (−) evaluation from the teacher based upon the student identifying a sufficient number of errors in a given examination.

H_1: The two groups are not from the same population and the experimental group will demonstrate better score reading ability than will the no-contact control group.

STUDY 4: N = 15, the total number of subjects

The purpose of this study was to determine if musical preference changes with *repeated* listenings. 15 students listened to *The Erlking* by Schubert and rated their preference (or like-dislike) on a one through seven scale. The preference was rated after the first, fourth, and 9th listenings.

H_1: The repeated observations are of different populations and music preference will decline with repeated listenings.

STUDY 5: N = 103, total number of students

One aspect of this study is to ascertain whether five groups (intended to be used as treatment groups) were drawn from the same population. All groups were given a pretest consisting of five subtests of the *Illinois Test of Psycholinguistic Ability*. The totalled score of these subtests was used as a basis of comparison between the subjects who will be members of five different treatment groups.

H_o: The groups are from the same population and there is no difference in the expected total of scores in each of the five groups.

STUDY 6: N = 30, total number of subjects

The purpose of this study was to determine the effect of special training on sight singing ability. Group A (15 subjects) was pre- and posttested. Group B (15 subjects) was pretested, given special instruction, and posttested. Pre- and posttesting consisted of a sight singing exercise with a possible score of ten points on each trial.

H_o: The samples are from the same population and there will be no difference in sight singing ability between the two groups.

STUDY 7: N = 30, total number of subjects

The purpose of this study was to test the effect of singing specially constructed music on speech articulation. Group 1 (15 subjects) received chanting in rhythm instruction. Group 2 (15 subjects) received singing of specially constructed music. Both groups were pre- and posttested. The two groups were *matched* on the basis of the pretest. Pre- and posttesting consisted of a tape recording of each subject's speech patterns analyzed by the voice spectrograph which gives duration of articulated sounds in hundredths of seconds.

H_1: The two groups are not from the same population and the chanting group will articulate less well than will the experimental group.

PRE/POSTTEST TO PROGRAM III
A Programmed Guide to Selected Research Designs

NOTE: The seven (7) sample studies referred to in this test are found at the end of the test.

1. Match the appropriate type of samples with the type of samples used in each study.

    Study 1 _____

    Study 2 _____   a. one-sample

    Study 3 _____   b. two-sample, equivalent

    Study 4 _____   c. two-sample, independent

    Study 5 _____   d. multiple-sample, equivalent

    Study 6 _____   e. multiple-sample, independent

    Study 7 _____

2. Write the symbols for:

    _____ treatment   _____ matching

    _____ measurement, or observation

3. Write in symbols the appropriate sequence of measurements and treatments used in the following studies:

    Study 1 _____   Study 6 _____

    Study 2 _____   Study 7 _____

    Study 3 _____

4. Match the appropriate level of measurement with the description of data given in each study:

    Study 1 _____   Study 6 _____

    Study 2 _____   Study 7 _____

    Study 3 _____   a. nominal

    Study 4 _____   b. ordinal

    Study 5 _____   c. interval or ratio

5. Match an appropriate statistical test with the data described in each study:

    Study 1 _____

    Study 2 _____   a. χ^2—*One Sample* test, especially good for data at nominal level.

    Study 4 _____   b. *McNemar Test for Sig. of Changes*, for use with two, equiv. samples when data are at nominal level.

    Study 6 _____   c. *Friedman Two-Way Analysis of Variance*, for multiple, equiv. samples—ordinal level.

    Study 7 _____   d. *Mann-Whitney U*, two indep. samples, ordinal level.

    e. *Parametric t-test*, one or two equiv. or indep. samples, data at the interval or ratio level.

6. Match the correct type of hypothesis with those given in the studies below:

Study 1 _____

Study 3 _____   a. one-tailed alternative hypothesis.

Study 4 _____   b. two-tailed alternative hypothesis.

Study 5 _____   c. Null Hypothesis.

Study 7 _____

7. Write a two-tailed alternative hypothesis for Study *2*:

_____

_____

_____

8. Write a one-tailed alternative hypothesis for Study *6*:

_____

_____

_____

9. Write a Null Hypothesis for Study *3*:

_____

_____

_____

10. Choose a significance level for Study *7*. Write the symbol and definition of significance level, and the rationale for your choice.

symbol for significance level = _____

significance level chosen = _____

definition of significance level:_____

_____

_____

Rationale for choice:_____

_____

_____

Studies

STUDY 1: N = 30, total number of subjects

This study attempts to determine which element of music is *cited* as reason for liking the piece of music on first hearing. 30 students listened to a piece of music and indicated their choice of tempo, rhythm, beat, melody, *or* form as their reason for liking the music.

H_o: The two groups are from the same population and there is no difference in the expected number of responses falling into each category.

STUDY 2: N = 24, total number of subjects

24 subjects received pretest, were matched on the basis of this and divided into two groups. Group 1 (12 subjects) received instruction about a new piece of music and a posttest. Group 2 (12 subjects) received no instruction and a posttest. The pre- and posttests were behavioral observations of whether the subjects were "on task" (+) or "off task" (−). The experimenter was interested in the effect of *analytical music instruction* about a new piece of music on the "on-off task" behavior of subjects listening to that piece of music.

H_o: The two groups are from the same population and there will be no difference in the mean amount of "on-task" behavior demonstrated.

STUDY 3: N = 16, the total number of subjects

This study was designed to evaluate programmed lessons in score reading. Eight subjects were used as a no-contact control group receiving no instruction in score reading. Eight subjects were used as an experimental group and read the programmed instruction in score reading. All 16 subjects were given a posttest consisting of a pass (+) or fail (−) evaluation from the teacher based upon the student identifying a sufficient number of errors in a given examination.

H_1: The two groups are not from the same population and the experimental group will demonstrate better score reading ability than will the no-contact control group.

STUDY 4: N = 15, the total number of subjects

The purpose of this study was to determine if musical preference changes with *repeated* listenings. 15 students listened to *The Erlking* by Schubert and rated their preference (or like-dislike) on a one through seven scale. The preference was rated after the first, fourth, and 9th listenings.

H_1: The repeated observations are of different populations and music preference will decline with repeated listenings.

STUDY 5: N = 103, total number of students

One aspect of this study is to ascertain whether five groups (intended to be used as treatment groups) were drawn from the same population. All groups were given a pretest consisting of five subtests of the *Illinois Test of Psycholinguistic Ability*. The totalled score of these subtests was used as a basis of comparison between the subjects who will be members of five different treatment groups.

H_o: The groups are from the same population and there is no difference in the expected total of scores in each of the five groups.

STUDY 6: N = 30, total number of subjects

The purpose of this study was to determine the effect of special training on sight singing ability. Group A (15 subjects) was pre- and posttested. Group B (15 subjects) was pretested, given special instruction, and posttested. Pre- and posttesting consisted of a sight singing exercise with a possible score of ten points on each trial.

H_o: The samples are from the same population and there will be no difference in sight singing ability between the two groups.

STUDY 7: N = 30, total number of subjects

The purpose of this study was to test the effect of singing specially constructed music on speech articulation. Group 1 (15 subjects) received chanting in rhythm instruction. Group 2 (15 subjects) received singing of specially constructed music. Both groups were pre- and posttested. The two groups were *matched* on the basis of the pretest. Pre- and posttesting consisted of a tape recording of each subject's speech patterns analyzed by the voice spectrograph which gives duration of articulated sounds in hundredths of seconds.

H_1: The two groups are not from the same population and the chanting group will articulate less well than will the experimental group.

PRE/POSTTEST TO PROGRAM IV
A Programmed Guide to Basic Statistics

I. *Match*

A. Random

B. Descriptive

C. Type I error

D. Mode

E. Inferential

F. Sampling

G. Median

H. Type II error

I. Mean

J. Range

K. Biased

L. Z score

1. only a few cases from a population are measured. *F*

2. difference between largest and smallest number in a set. *J*

3. commonly known as the "average." *I*

4. every member has an equal and independent chance of being chosen. *A*

5. probability of rejecting a true null hypothesis. *H* / *C*

6. probability of not rejecting a false null hypothesis. *H* *C*

7. the score in the middle of a set. *G*

8. statistic which generalizes from a small set to a population. *E*

9. every member chosen from a set for a common characteristic. *K*

10. statistic which accounts for a group of data. *B*

11. score transformed linearly to a normal curve distribution. *L*

12. score most frequently found in a set of data points. *D*

II. 2 4 5 5 5 6 8 9

Given this sample from a population, find the following (when $\Sigma X = 44$ and $N = 8$):

Median 5

Mode 5

Range 7

Mean 5.5

III. If the variance (s^2) is given, what are the corresponding standard deviations(s)?

$s^2 = 36, s = \underline{6}$ $\qquad\qquad$ $s^2 = 100, s = \underline{10}$

When a standard deviation is given, find the variance:

$s = 5, s^2 = \underline{25}$ $\qquad\qquad$ $s = 8, s^2 = \underline{64}$

Given the variance of a set of scores is 16, what is the variance when each score has five added to it.

$s^2 = \underline{16}$

153

IV. The standard deviation of a distribution is a measure of the _____variation_____ of the scores in the distribution; while the mean of a distribution is a measure of the _____central tendency_____ of the scores in the distribution.

    A.   location
    B.   variation
    C.   central tendency

    D.   skewness
    E.   none of these

V. For the following set of data points, find the *mean, variance,* and *standard deviation* (when $\Sigma\chi = 40, \Sigma\chi^2 = 264, N = 8$):

    1 2 3 5 5 6 8 10

    $\overline{X} = $ _____5_____

    $s^2 = $ _____9.14_____

    $s = $ _____3.02_____

(handwritten work at right)
-4 16
-3 9
-2 4
0
0
1 1
3 9
5 25

64 / 7 = 9.14

VI. A distribution of scores with mean = 20 and variance = 25, what is the standard score (Z score) corresponding to a raw score of 15? (Remember $Z = \dfrac{X - \overline{X}}{s}$)

    A. +0.20
    B. +1.00
    (C.) −1.00

    D. −0.20
    E. none of these

(handwritten) $\dfrac{15-20}{\sqrt{25}\ 5}$

VII.

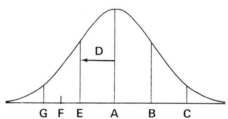

    G F E   A   B   C

Which letter marks the mean? A

Which letter signifies the standard deviation? D

Which letter represents −1.00? E

Which letter marks 0 (zero)? A

Which letter represents +2.00? C

Which letter identifies −1.50? F

VIII. Given the following distribution: 1, 6, 11, find the following:

    $\overline{X} = $ _____6_____

    $s^2 = $ _____25_____

    $s = $ _____5_____

(handwritten)
-5 25
0
5 25

50 / 2 = 25

$\overline{X} = 75 \qquad SD = 15$

IX. A musical aptitude test was given to all third grade classes in the state of Florida. The mean score on this test was 75 and the standard deviation of the children's scores was 15 points. Suppose that the classes are composed of 36 children each, so that in effect there are a vast number of samples of 36 scores each.

Draw and label the graph of the distribution of the means of these samples, assuming that each sample is a random collection of 36 scores. (Remember that $s_{\bar{x}} = \frac{s}{\sqrt{N}}$)   Find $s_{\bar{x}}$

$$\frac{15}{6}$$

$$s_{\bar{x}} = 2.5$$

X. Following the above question (IX),

A.   In what *percent* of the classes would we expect the class mean to be as high as 80? (use Normal Curve Table)

B.   In what percent would the mean be as low as 70?

$\overline{X}$

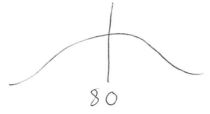

80

80

PRE/POSTTEST TO PROGRAM IV
A Programmed Guide to Basic Statistics

I. *Match*

A. Random

B. Descriptive

C. Type I error

D. Mode

E. Inferential

F. Sampling

G. Median

H. Type II error

I. Mean

J. Range

K. Biased

L. Z score

1. only a few cases from a population are measured.

2. difference between largest and smallest number in a set.

3. commonly known as the "average."

4. every member has an equal and independent chance of being chosen.

5. probability of rejecting a true null hypothesis.

6. probability of not rejecting a false null hypothesis.

7. the score in the middle of a set.

8. statistic which generalizes from a small set to a population.

9. every member chosen from a set for a common characteristic.

10. statistic which accounts for a group of data.

11. score transformed linearly to a normal curve distribution.

12. score most frequently found in a set of data points.

II. 2   4   5   5   5   6   8   9

Given this sample from a population, find the following (when $\Sigma X = 44$ and $N = 8$):

Median

Mode

Range

Mean

III. If the variance (s^2) is given, what are the corresponding standard deviations(s)?

$s^2 = 36, s = $ _____ $s^2 = 100, s = $ _____

When a standard deviation is given, find the variance:

$s = 5, s^2 = $ _____ $s = 8, s^2 = $ _____

Given the variance of a set of scores is 16, what is the variance when each score has five added to it.

$s^2 = $ _____

IV. The standard deviation of a distribution is a measure of the _____ of the scores in the distribution; while the mean of a distribution is a measure of the _____ of the scores in the distribution.

A. location
B. variation
C. central tendency

D. skewness
E. none of these

V. For the following set of data points, find the *mean, variance,* and *standard deviation* (when $\Sigma X = 40, \Sigma X^2 = 264, N = 8$):

1 2 3 5 5 6 8 10

$\overline{X}$ = _____

s^2 = _____

s = _____

VI. A distribution of scores with mean = 20 and variance = 25, what is the standard score (Z score) corresponding to a raw score of 15? (Remember $Z = \dfrac{X - \overline{X}}{s}$)

A. +0.20
B. +1.00
C. −1.00

D. −0.20
E. none of these

VII.

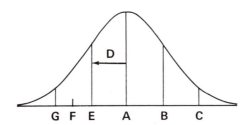

Which letter marks the mean?

Which letter signifies the standard deviation?

Which letter represents −1.00?

Which letter marks 0 (zero)?

Which letter represents +2.00?

Which letter identifies −1.50?

VIII. Given the following distribution: 1, 6, 11, find the following:

$\overline{X}$ = _____

s^2 = _____

s = _____

IX. A musical aptitude test was given to all third grade classes in the state of Florida. The mean score on this test was 75 and the standard deviation of the children's scores was 15 points. Suppose that the classes are composed of 36 children each, so that in effect there are a vast number of samples of 36 scores each.

Draw and label the graph of the distribution of the means of these samples, assuming that each sample is a random collection of 36 scores. (Remember that $s_{\bar{x}} = \frac{s}{\sqrt{N}}$) Find $s_{\bar{x}}$

X. Following the above question (IX),

A. In what *percent* of the classes would we expect the class mean to be as high as 80? (use Normal Curve Table)

B. In what percent would the mean be as low as 70?

PRE/POSTTEST V
A Programmed Guide to Statistical Tests

I. *Match*

   A. χ^2 One Sample.

   B. χ^2 Two Sample-Dependent.

   C. χ^2 Two Sample-Independent.

   D. Wilcoxon Matched-Pairs Signed Ranks.

   E. Mann-Whitney U

   F. Friedman Two-Way Analysis of Variance.

   G. Kruskal-Wallis One-Way Analysis of Variance.

   H. Dunn's Multiple Comparison Procedure.

   I. t Test.

   J. F test, One-Way Analysis of Variance.

   K. Newman-Keuls Multiple Comparison Procedure.

   L. Pearson Product Moment.

   M. Spearman Rank Correlation.

Answer

_____ 1. compares sum of rank scores among k groups.

_____ 2. determines if two independent groups are drawn from same population by comparing sum of ranks.

_____ 3. "Goodness of fit," how obtained value fits expected value.

_____ 4. compares means of two groups taking into account the variances and assumes homogeneity and normality.

_____ 5. used following Kruskal-Wallis to determine if two group means differ.

_____ 6. measures degree of association between two sets of scores which are ranked separately.

_____ 7. determine significant changes in two related categories; often subject used as own control or in before-after design.

_____ 8. relationship between two sets of data by assuming linearity, continuous and interval data.

_____ 9. compare k means by using a ratio of variances; assumes sample is taken from a normal distribution.

_____ 10. difference in two independent samples over two or more conditions for nominal data.

_____ 11. analyze rank signs of difference scores of two matched groups.

_____ 12. compare k matched samples of equal size by summing ranks.

_____ 13. compare k means which are ordered in size (follows F test).

II. *Multiple-Choice.*

A. If a sample is made up of people, each of whom had an equal and independent chance of being chosen from the population, the sample is said to be:

1. random sample
2. biased sample
3. stratified sample

B. The value of a sample statistic must contain evidence about the value of the corresponding population value, and a central problem in inferential statistics is the use of sample statistics as estimators of population values. Since a single value $(\overline{X})$ is taken as the estimate, it is most properly called:

1. random sample
2. point estimate
3. interval estimate

4. standard error
5. standard deviation

C. Which of the following scatter diagrams of the relationship between a variable X and a variable Y would enable a researcher to make the most accurate prediction of one of the variables from a knowledge of the other?

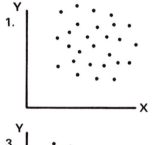

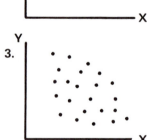

D. For each of the diagrams in question C above, describe the relationship using the terms: negative, zero, and positive.

1. _____ 3. _____

2. _____ 4. _____

E. A researcher is trying to predict Z_y' when $Z_x = +1.00$. Given the regression equation $Z_y' = r Z_x$ and $r = +0.80$, which of the following would be the most accurate prediction?

1. +0.64
2. +1.00
3. +0.80
4. −0.80

III. *Identify*

Tell which statistical test would be used for each of the following problems:

A. Two independent groups of violin students from two neighboring high schools have difficulty playing dotted rhythms accurately. Group A is given a dotted rhythm exercise from a standard method book with neuromuscular exercises to improve rhythmic performance. Group B is given the same standard exercise while imitating the teacher's model. All students tape a posttest performance of the given exercise.

Posttest Results: (correct responses)	Group A	Group B
	46	43
	25	40
	30	22
	37	24
	32	30
	48	50
		42
		19
		12
		8

B. A group of grade school children were asked which of four television programs they liked best. The four programs were: an educational program, a cartoon show, an adventure series, and a concert series for children. Evaluate the hypothesis that the four programs are equally preferred.

| | Program: | | | |
	Educational	Cartoon	Adventure	Music
Frequency of preference:	40	60	50	30

C. A school psychologist wanted to know if a test of musical appreciation would predict musical ability. Scores on the test were designated "high," "medium," or "low," and ability was independently assessed by a music teacher. Is there evidence in the data for the association of the two variables?

| | Ability | | | |
	Poor	Average	Good	Exceptional
high	9	11	21	10
medium	7	36	31	8
low	15	21	7	8

D. Six students missed the following number of problems on a music test and a math test. Is there any linear relationship?

Music test scores: 7 8 7 5 7 2

Math test scores: 2 3 8 3 3 5

IV. *Computation.*

Compute problem A and/or B from Question III. Give the following information:

    1. H_o:

       df:

    2. Computation of Problem (check workbook for formula and tables).

    3. The obtained value = _____

       The tabled critical value = _____

    4. Assuming .05 level of significance, make the appropriate statistical decision:

    5. Finally, state the experimental decision:

PRE/POSTTEST V
A Programmed Guide to Statistical Tests

I. *Match*

A. χ^2 One Sample.

B. χ^2 Two Sample-Dependent.

C. χ^2 Two Sample-Independent.

D. Wilcoxon Matched-Pairs Signed Ranks.

E. Mann-Whitney U

F. Friedman Two-Way Analysis of Variance.

G. Kruskal-Wallis One-Way Analysis of Variance.

H. Dunn's Multiple Comparison Procedure.

I. t Test.

J. F test, One-Way Analysis of Variance.

K. Newman-Keuls Multiple Comparison Procedure.

L. Pearson Product Moment.

M. Spearman Rank Correlation.

Answer

_____ 1. compares sum of rank scores among k groups.

_____ 2. determines if two independent groups are drawn from same population by comparing sum of ranks.

_____ 3. "Goodness of fit," how obtained value fits expected value.

_____ 4. compares means of two groups taking into account the variances and assumes homogeneity and normality.

_____ 5. used following Kruskal-Wallis to determine if two group means differ.

_____ 6. measures degree of association between two sets of scores which are ranked separately.

_____ 7. determine significant changes in two related categories; often subject used as own control or in before-after design.

_____ 8. relationship between two sets of data by assuming linearity, continuous and interval data.

_____ 9. compare k means by using a ratio of variances; assumes sample is taken from a normal distribution.

_____ 10. difference in two independent samples over two or more conditions for nominal data.

_____ 11. analyze rank signs of difference scores of two matched groups.

_____ 12. compare k matched samples of equal size by summing ranks.

_____ 13. compare k means which are ordered in size (follows F test).

II. *Multiple-Choice.*

A. If a sample is made up of people, each of whom had an equal and independent chance of being chosen from the population, the sample is said to be:

   1. random sample
   2. biased sample
   3. stratified sample

B. The value of a sample statistic must contain evidence about the value of the corresponding population value, and a central problem in inferential statistics is the use of sample statistics as estimators of population values. Since a single value $(\overline{X})$ is taken as the estimate, it is most properly called:

   1. random sample   4. standard error
   2. point estimate   5. standard deviation
   3. interval estimate

C. Which of the following scatter diagrams of the relationship between a variable X and a variable Y would enable a researcher to make the most accurate prediction of one of the variables from a knowledge of the other?

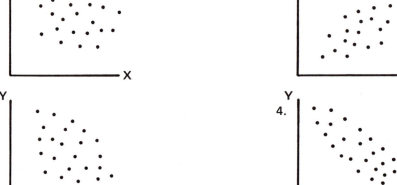

D. For each of the diagrams in question C above, describe the relationship using the terms: negative, zero, and positive.

   1. _____   3. _____
   2. _____   4. _____

E. A researcher is trying to predict Z_y' when $Z_x = +1.00$. Given the regression equation $Z_y' = r\, Z_x$ and $r = +0.80$, which of the following would be the most accurate prediction?

   1. +0.64
   2. +1.00
   3. +0.80
   4. −0.80

III. *Identify*

Tell which statistical test would be used for each of the following problems:

A. Two independent groups of violin students from two neighboring high schools have difficulty playing dotted rhythms accurately. Group A is given a dotted rhythm exercise from a standard method book with neuromuscular exercises to improve rhythmic performance. Group B is given the same standard exercise while imitating the teacher's model. All students tape a posttest performance of the given exercise.

Posttest Results: (correct responses)	Group A	Group B
	46	43
	25	40
	30	22
	37	24
	32	30
	48	50
		42
		19
		12
		8

B. A group of grade school children were asked which of four television programs they liked best. The four programs were: an educational program, a cartoon show, an adventure series, and a concert series for children. Evaluate the hypothesis that the four programs are equally preferred.

	Program:			
	Educational	Cartoon	Adventure	Music
Frequency of preference:	40	60	50	30

C. A school psychologist wanted to know if a test of musical appreciation would predict musical ability. Scores on the test were designated "high," "medium," or "low," and ability was independently assessed by a music teacher. Is there evidence in the data for the association of the two variables?

	Ability			
	Poor	Average	Good	Exceptional
high	9	11	21	10
medium	7	36	31	8
low	15	21	7	8

D. Six students missed the following number of problems on a music test and a math test. Is there any linear relationship?

Music test scores: 7 8 7 5 7 2

Math test scores: 2 3 8 3 3 5

IV. *Computation.*

Compute problem A and/or B from Question III. Give the following information:

1. H_o:

   df:

2. Computation of Problem (check workbook for formula and tables).

3. The obtained value = _____

   The tabled critical value = _____

4. Assuming .05 level of significance, make the appropriate statistical decision:

5. Finally, state the experimental decision:

EXPERIMENTAL RESEARCH IN MUSIC:
WORKBOOK IN DESIGN AND STATISTICAL TESTS*
ANSWERS TO PRE/POSTTESTS I-V

Pre/Posttest I   A Programmed Guide to Closed Systems

1. A closed system is a group of objects, symbols, or ideas which are intrinsically consistent but are extrinsically invalid.

2. *Set*

3. *Transfer*

4. Mode of inquiry is a particular way of thinking about a subject or idea; it may represent a point of view. In music, three modes of inquiry might be those of composer, conductor and performer.

5. Four closed systems in reading music might include:

   a. clef
   b. key signature
   c. tempo
   d. meter signature

6. Phenomenological   4. A / B C
   Assumptive   1. A ∴ B C
   Hypothetical   5. (A)   B C ∴ A

7. Ten closed systems on a musical score:

   a. title
   b. opus number
   c. orchestration
   d. composer's name
   e. (date)
   f. tempo marking in Italian
   g. dynamic marks (P)
   h. articulation term (pizz.)
   i. rests
   j. notation

Pre/Posttest II   A Programmed Guide to Mill's Canons

1. John Stuart Mill was a nineteenth century philosopher who formulated five guidelines, or "canons," for systematically pinpointing the causes of events.

2. The rationale of Mill's Canons holds that if the cause of an event can be determined, an experimental design could be created for study of that event.

3. The importance of Mill's Canons to the beginning experimenter in music is that they provide a verbal rationale for designing an experiment.

4. Mill's Method of Agreement proposes that if the circumstances leading up to a given event have in every case *only one common factor*, that factor is probably the cause.

5. Mill's Method of Differences proposes that if two or more sets of circumstances are alike in every respect except for one factor and if a given event occurs only when that factor is present, the factor in question probably is the cause of that event.

*These tests are in pilot form. While they have been administered and subsequently analyzed many times, they are still being evaluated and should be used with caution. In an attempt to further refine these instruments and increase the total number of respondents we encourage you to send completed forms to:

Randall S. Moore
School of Music
University of Oregon
Eugene, Oregon 97403

6. Mill's Joint Method combines the Agreement and Difference Methods in that one factor common to an occurrence is found and then the factor is withdrawn to determine if the phenomenon occurs only when the factor is present.

7. The Method of Residues proposes that when the specific factors causing certain parts of a given phenomenon are known, the remaining parts of the phenomenon must be caused by the remaining factors.

8. Mill's Method of Concomitant variation proposes that when two things consistently change or vary together, either the variations in one are caused by the variations in the other, or both are being affected by some common cause.

9. Method of Differences.

10. Joint Method.

11. Method of Agreement.

12. Concomitant Variations.

13. Method of Residues.

Mill's Canons

1.	D	7.	E
2.	A	8.	B
3.	C	9.	C
4.	E	10.	E
5.	D	11.	D
6.	A	12.	A

Pre/Posttest III   A Programmed Guide to Selected Research Designs

(1) Study 1 __a__

Study 2 __b__

Study 3 __c__

Study 4 __d(a)__

Study 5 __e__

Study 6 __c__

Study 7 __b__

(2)

$\underline{X}$ treatment

$\underline{O}$ measurement

$\underline{M}$ matching

(3) Study 1 __$O_1 O_2$__

Study 2 __$O_1 M$ $\begin{array}{c} X \ O_2 \\ O_2 \end{array}$__

Study 3 __$\begin{array}{c} X \ O_1 \\ O_1 \end{array}$__

Study 6 __$\begin{array}{c} O_1 \ X \ O_2 \\ O_1 \quad O_2 \end{array}$__

Study 7 __$(O)M \begin{array}{c} X_1 \ O \\ X_2 \ O \end{array}$__

(4) Study 1 __a__

Study 2 __a__

Study 3 __a__

Study 4 __b__

Study 5 __c(b)__

Study 6 __b__

Study 7 __c__

170

(5) Study 1   <u>a(b)</u>

Study 2   <u>b</u>

Study 4   <u>c b</u>

Study 5   <u>d</u>

Study 7   <u>e</u>

(6) Study 1   <u>c</u>   Study 5   <u>c</u>

Study 3   <u>a</u>   Study 7   <u>a</u>

Study 4   <u>a</u>

(7) H_1 : The two groups are not from the same population and there will be a difference in the mean amount of "on-task" behavior demonstrated.

(8) H_1 : The samples are not from the same population and Group B which was given special instruction will be significantly higher in sight singing ability.

(9) H_0 : The two groups are from the same population and there will be no difference in score reading ability between both groups.

(10) Symbol for significance level $= \alpha$

Significance level chosen $= .05$

Definition of significance level: *95% sure that findings did not occur by chance alone.*

Rationale for choice: *Spectrograph analysis may be highly accurate but the two methods employed do not differ sufficiently to set a lower significance level. Also, the study is not a vitally critical issue.*

Answers to Pre/Posttest IV   A Programmed Guide to Basic Statistics

I.   1. F   5. H   9. K
        2. J   6. C   10. B
        3. I   7. G   11. L
        4. A   8. E   12. D

II.   Median = 5   Mode = 5   Range = 7   Mean = 5.5

III. $s^2 = 36$, $s = \underline{6}$ $s^2 = 100$, $s = \underline{10}$
      $s = 5$, $s^2 = \underline{25}$ $s = 8$, $s^2 = \underline{64}$
      $s^2 = \underline{16}$

IV.   <u>B</u>   <u>C</u>

V. $\overline{X} = \underline{5}$ $s^2 = \underline{9.143}$ $s = \underline{3.028}$

VI.   C. $\underline{-1.00}$

VII.   Mean <u>A</u>   Standard Deviation <u>D</u> -1.00 <u>E</u>
      Zero <u>A</u> $+2.00$ <u>C</u> -1.50 <u>F</u>

VIII. $\overline{X}$ = <u>6</u> s^2 = <u>25</u>   s = <u>5</u>

IX.   (a) $s_{\overline{X}}$ = <u>2.5</u>   IX.   (b)

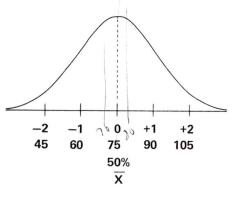

X.   (a) Upper <u>40%</u>   (b) Lower <u>40%</u>

| -2 | -1 | 0 | +1 | +2 |
| 45 | 60 | 75 | 90 | 105 |

50%
$\overline{X}$

Answers to Pre/Posttest V   A Programmed Guide to Statistical Tests

I.   1. G   8. L
        2. E   9. J
        3. A   10. C
        4. I   11. D
        5. H   12. F
        6. M   13. K
        7. B

II. A. *1*
     B. *2*
     C. *2*
     D. 1. *Zero*
         2. *positive*
         3. *negative*
         4. *high negative*
     E. *3*

III. A. *Mann-Whitney U*
      B. χ^2 *one-sample*
      C. χ^2 *two-sample independent*
      D. *Pearson Product Moment Correlation*

IV. A. for Problem A:
         1. H_o: *No difference*
             α = *.05 (two-tailed)*
         2. *U* = *19.5* (obtained value)
         3. tabled value *U* = *11*
         4. *Not reject H_o*
         5. *No significant effect with neuro-muscular exercise or teacher's model, i.e., one is not any better or different from the other.*

for Problem B:
         1. H_o: *No difference between choices, or all preferences are equal. df = 3*
         2. χ^2 = *11.1* (obtained value)
         3. tabled value χ^2 = *7.82*
         4. *Reject H_o*
         5. *Preferences are different*